Published by MTNWalker Media, L.L.C.
6080 South Hulen, Suite 360, PMB 101
Fort Worth, Texas 76132

AlexisFaere.com

ISBN 978-1-958786-12-3

Graceful Whispers: 365 Wonder-Filled Prayers for Grandpa

A Year of Delightful Conversations With God.

Dedicated to my Grandpa...
a disciplined shepherd

Thank you for sharing these
prayers with me, so that we could
have a little time together each day.

Start anywhere in the book and use
it every year to stay connected with
each of your hearts.

Backward ...
(Forward...)

My Grandparents were gracious, loving people, and well-established in their traditional Christian beliefs. I saw many gaps between their 'way of life' and mine.

For most of our lives, many miles separated my Grandparents and me. As they aged, and as more permanent daily care was required for them, there was a part of me that got sensitive to that distance. It was a distance that somehow longed for closer proximity. I felt deeply about the changes they were facing, and I wanted to be supportive and loving in the best way I knew how.

My creative approach to this was to write a daily ditty, if you will, that would give my Grandparents, my Grandma and my Grandpa, a moment of personal time with me each day. So I set out to create a personal book for each of them. This book, *Graceful Whispers* is the Grandpa version of this book. I've also released the Grandma version called *Whispers of Love*.

The moments contained in these pages are filled with understanding, joy, fun, and the topics are introspective. I invited my grandparents into my inner world using a language they could relate to.

These thoughts, in a simple prayer format, were intended to be presented in a language they appreciated and understood. This allowed me to lay a framework for us to share with each other, to connect and respect one another in ways that we had not yet connected.

Remember, I wrote this to be received by a person who had a belief system that was, shall we say, more stringent, perhaps, than my own. So while the references to 'God', 'Savior', and so on, may not be your own personal favorite references, it is intended to be a prayer offered—however you may offer your own prayers, to whomever you may offer them.

Perhaps you've gifted this offering, as a Grandchild, to your own Grandfather. I offer these moments each day, for years on end, if wished; for a Grandchild to relate to a Grandparent in a kind, loving, supportive, and adventurous manner.

Enjoy these moments, and may your relationships grow and be blessed...

January 1

Hey God,

Today we're stepping into a brand new year.
As Grandpa enjoys his daily rituals, and maybe even a
black-eyed pea, or apples and honey,
please watch over him.

Bless this day. Pave the way for the New Year
so that he finds at least 2 or 3 blessings in each day.

While you're at it, please touch his heart so he knows
how much I love him. He is important to me and to
others. Help him know how much he matters—
to me and to others.

January 2

Abundant Provider...

Your warm sunshine makes us good wheat,
potatoes, corn, tomatoes, and onions.

Thank you for these amazing creations
which nourish our bodies and make it
possible for me to have a Grandpa.

Thank you for being sure I have a Grandpa
who cares, who loves, and who prays.

January 3

Heavenly Father,

Grandpa is so very resourceful. How many countless things did he build to help his family? I have a chair he built for my Dad when he was a boy. I still use that chair today.

Grandpa had no idea when he built a chair that his creation would be used decades later. That's kind of like we are to you—you make us, and we are still useful decades later. Can you please let Grandpa know how useful he is to you today?

January 4

Dear Lord,

You touch all of life and that means you've been part of my Grandpa's life every day that he has lived.

Thank you.

Before he was my Grandpa, you led him through experiences that make him who he is today.

Thank you.

Thank you for opening my heart so I can love my Grandpa.

Peacefully...

January 5

It's me, God.

Grandpa taught me how to be methodical
in my search for solutions.

Thank you for making him so methodical so he
could teach me about it. When he putters
around in his workshop today, would you
please let him know how magical he is?

He's my Grandpa, and he's magical to me.
Magically methodical...

January 6

Oh, Dear God,

This morning, I woke up grumpy!
I bet Grandpa has grumpy days, too.

When he does, can you make him aware
that it's okay to have grumpy days?
And they don't have to last forever?

Perplexed...

January 7

Great healing and nurturing God,

Sometimes Grandpa doesn't feel like his chipper self. When he doesn't feel up to par, I wonder if you could envelop him with your cradling and nurturing hands.

Even grandpas like to be held and nurtured. He cared enough to give me a bandaid when I cut my finger once—I'd like to know that Grandpa is cared for, too.

Thank you for handling Grandpa with caring.

January 8

Good morning, Lord,

Thanks for that bright, beaming sunshine you give us.
I like how your bright light colors the sky
even when there are clouds.

When I see and feel this sunshine, I imagine it reaches
out and touches my Grandpa, and shines on his
home, filling him with warmth and hope.

Adventurously...

January 9

Be careful, God.

Grandpa likes to play Yahtzee.

When we play together, and someone is about to throw a Yahtzee, he always says "Be careful!"

Maybe Grandpa is about to do something and he needs to be careful. Can you watch over him today?

Carefully...

January 10

It's me again, God,

I'm sure you're aware Grandpa takes time to pray every day.
When he prays today, will you remind him that I love him?

He is faith-full and loyal, and I love him for that. When he asks for something, remember he comes to you in faith.

Faithfully...

January 11

Amazing and Graceful God,

Yaaaaawn.
That sure was a good night's sleep last night.

I hope Grandpa got some good rest
last night. Thank you for watching over him,
so when he wakes up, he feels spunky
and ready for the gift of a new day.

I know your Grace protects him from harm.
Thank you.

Creatively...

January 12

Hello God.

Today someone tapped me on the shoulder.
Grandpa always has wise things to
share that guide me in my life.

I think that tap was Grandpa's gentle touch
—encouraging me on my way.

For Grandpa's gentle touches,
thank you, Dear Lord.

January 13

God,

When Grandpa thinks of his family today,
help him remember something about
each one that helps him smile.

When Grandpa smiles, his eyes twinkle.

I'm pretty sure those twinkles
come from you.

Smiling...

January 14

Tender and Loving God,

Our eyes allow us to see, cry, and laugh.
When I cry, I know your hand is there to
guide me.

When Grandpa cries, will you let him
know his tears are blessings that help his
spirit and heart to grow?

Thank you for your comfort.

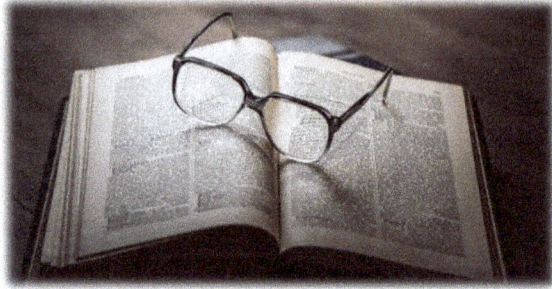

January 15

I was wondering, Father,

When Grandpa remembers a story about his life, could you remind him how special he is?

Grandpa's stories are special to me. I'm grateful he shares stories with me about growing up, and silly things he did as a kid.

I'm grateful I have Grandpa stories to share. (Grandpas are important people.)

Shared stories...

January 16

Wonderous Lord,

Icicles are magical.
Icicles melt and change the way they look.
They don't last forever, either. They come
and share their beauty, and then they melt
away to nourish the land beneath them.

Grandpas are kind of like that, too.

They help to make our lives beautiful,
and then one day, they return to the
earth to nourish our world.

You are always there, surrounding us and
protecting us, even as we change.
Thank you for your watchful eye.

Bewildered...

January 17

Powerful and Loving God,

You are a vast wonderment, and we know so very little about you. Sometimes we realize how little we know about ourselves.

Today, would you open Grandpa's heart so he learns something about himself today?

When he learns about himself, his soul grows. Your guiding hands help us learn more about you and ourselves.

Searching...

January 18

Psssst! God!

On this day, could you guide someone to touch Grandpa's hand so that he knows your presence?

Grandpa is experiencing a new day today, just like me. I'd really like it if you could open his heart to something really special today.

Thanks, God.

January 19

Okay God.

We've started on our journey for this New Year.
Walk with my Grandpa as his days unfold
and his life continues to blossom.

Walk with him today where he
roams and where he rests.

Help him recognize 3 gifts from you today.

Abundantly...

January 20

Nourishing Savior,

Grandpa loves to go get a hamburger
to eat now and then. I think
hamburgers make him feel young.

Whether he is having a hamburger or a
corny dog today, can you please help his
heart to feel young and vibrant?

Youthfully...

January 21

Hello, Lord Jesus.

I wonder if Grandpa remembers any of his teachers.

You know, it's probably been a while since
Grandpa thought of a teacher in his life.

As he remembers a teacher that touched his life, let
us all remember the teachers we have in each day.

We're learning, Lord.

January 22

Here we go, Lord.

Everyday someone special says a prayer for Grandpa.

Whatever he needs, whatever he wants, could you just let him know of your guiding presence?

Let an angel fill his heart today, and let angels go with him wherever he goes.

Watchfully...

January 23

Father,

Thank you for letting Grandpa
hear our prayers for him.

He is an amazing person—
this man I call Grandpa.

Help him feel full-filled as he
says his blessings today.

Prayerfully...

January 24

Our Father, who art in Heaven, hallowed be thy name.

Thy kingdom come, thy will be done,
on earth as it is in heaven.

Give us this day, our daily bread,
and forgive those who aren't always kind to us.

Lead us not into temptation and deliver us from evil.

For Thine is the Kingdom,
the Power and the Glory forever.

Amen.

January 25

Playful One,

How long has it been since Grandpa remembered something fun he did as a child?

Could you spark a memory that fills his heart with laughter?

(I hope his belly wiggles when he remembers.)

Grandpa could use a good giggle today. Giggles help us remember joy.

Thank you for the way our hearts tickle when we giggle.

January 26

Wow!

Grandpa loves me. God, you are indeed exuberant. Your gracious love reaches out and touches me through many loving gestures from my Grandpa.

He took time to read books with me when I was just a wee one; he took me on camping trips; he took walks with me; and he says a prayer for me each day.

Thank you for all the ways Grandpa says I love you.

Exuberantly...

January 27

Hey God,

You must really enjoy watching us live our lives.

I say that because you give us mountains and streams and other people for us to share our lives with.

Grandpa is always generous when he shares himself with me.

I thank you, Grandpa.

God Bless our lives today!

January 28

Dear Heavenly Father,

Honorably...

January 29

Creative Lord,

What an amazing thing you do each day—
creating new days with sunrises and sunsets.

Your art upon the heavens is a blessing.
All we need to do is notice.

I like the way you make it so that Grandpa
and I both have a sky to behold, and
yet each one is different.

May your sky paintings give him a feeling of
hope, and may he sense the love of his family
as he travels through this day.

Amazed...

January 30

Hello God.

It's me. Did you see my thoughts about my
Grandpa today?
I thought—I wonder if he's drinking his coffee.

Perhaps he's having some personal worship
time. I wonder if he's visiting with Grandma.

Is he going to read the paper today?
I wonder if he's talking with his friend today.

Thank you for the gift of this day.

January 31

I was thinking, Lord,

Grandpa is always good at fixing things.
Life is complex sometimes, and we just need a
fix-it guy to help us tend to some of our challenges.

If Grandpa needs something fixed,
could you step in and lend him a hand?

Touching up...

February 1

Dear Lord Jesus,

You touch my Grandpa's life every day.

Thank you.

Before he was even my Grandpa, you led him through
the experiences that make him who he is today.

Thank you.

Thank you for opening my heart
so I can love my Grandpa.

Peacefully...

February 2

Well God,

I sure am loving my Grandpa today.
Would you please let him know?

There is strength in my soul because
I'm part of this wonderful Grandpa.

There are beams of strength between us. I'm
pretending there are highways of strength from my
heart to his—all day long and through the night.

Thank you for your strength!

February 3

A quick thought, Oh Lord.

I love Grandpa.

You're awesome!

February 4

God?

Grandpa lives far away from me. I ask you to protect him today. Protect his house.

Watch over him as he makes his way through the day today. If he needs warmth, let him know warmth.

If he needs inspiration, let him be aware of your presence as you gently provide those ideas.

Thank you, for touching Grandpa today...

February 5

It's me again, God.

Thank you for being there every day, Lord. I'm comforted to know that you're always watching over Grandpa—that way he's never alone.

It is my prayer, Dear Lord, that Grandpa feels your presence in whatever way is best for him today.

You're constant and sure...

February 6

Dear Master Creator,

Wow! It's already February.

The year is moving right along. As
Grandpa's year continues to live
and grow, let his soul understand
that my soul loves him dearly.

May this year continue to
be full of blessings.

Thank you, Lord.

February 7

Dear God,

Grandpa reads the paper almost every day.
As he learns about things going on in the
world, help him remember to be gracious
and know that you're keeping us all in your
heart. Also, can you help him find good
news in the paper that he can celebrate?

Let's celebrate good news...

February 8

Hey God,

There's a rabbit in the woods that could use a hand. Touch all your creatures today and guide them through the life that is theirs today (including Grandpa).

With wonder...

February 9

Patient Spirit,

When I was much younger, Grandpa sometimes lost his patience with me. You must lose your patience with us sometimes, too.

We're like little seeds growing into solid rooted plants, and sometimes we want to hurry things up a bit.

Grandpa's doing the best he can. Can you grant him patience to get where he needs to be?

Lovingly...

February 10

Well God,

I'm feeling so very sleepy today. I
bet Grandpa has sleepy days, too.
It's nice to take a nap when we feel
sleepy, but sometimes we can't.

If Grandpa is feeling sleepy and
needs a boost of energy, maybe you
could give him a quick splash of
alertness for his task.

Thanks for the spark!

February 11

Hey you. God,

Sometimes I feel like nobody sees me. I'm here, and
there are people around, but I don't feel seen. Can you
please be sure Grandpa knows he is seen and loved?

If someone passes him by and he feels unnoticed,
help him know you see him.

You have the best glasses...

February 12

Pssst! God!

What is Grandpa thinking about right now?
His thoughts are his to share when he is ready.

If he seeks guidance, please provide.
Maybe he's thinking about the state of our
world and has concerns. Perhaps you could
guide our leaders in their choices and decisions.

Whatever his thoughts are, let Grandpa
know he is not alone.

Thoughtfully...

February 13

God?

You know when your sunshine feels
like a warm blanket?

Could you help Grandpa feel that cuddly warmth
sometime today? Sometimes the days are rather cold
and that sunshine warmth surely does a body good.

Here's a warm hug from me to Grandpa.
Thanks for helping him to feel my hugs.

Warmly...

February 14

Dear Lord,

Someone spoke crossly to me today. It stung me to
my very core. Does that ever happen to Grandpa?
If someone does that to him, please help him
understand where that sting is coming from.

Sometimes cross words help us learn about
ourselves, and sometimes they are cries
from the other person for help.

Watching and listening...

February 15

God?

I'm remembering a meadow I saw on a hike.
It was green with grass and other
plants, and there was a generous
smattering of wild flowers.

Your wildflowers are one of the many ways
you smile upon us. Can you show Grandpa
something that makes him aware that
you are smiling upon him?

Aware and breathing...

February 16

Time for a chat, God.

Thank you for talking. We have so many ways to talk with each other. Thank you for the telephone, the letters, the visits, the conversations that grace my Grandpa's life.

Thank you, God, for talking with us, and listening with us, so that we might learn more about who we are in your world. I enjoy talking with you about Grandpa.

Thank you for conversations.

February 17

Bountiful Savior,

I'm grateful Grandpa has a place to call home. I'm glad he has shelter, a warm bed to sleep in at night, and a place to hang his hat. As Grandpa makes his journey through this day, help him know that his home is a blessing and that you care about him.

Graciously....

February 18

Wondrous Father,

As Grandpa has gotten older, sometimes his thoughts are not as clear as they once were. I know his thoughts are still good though.

Whatever Grandpa's thoughts are and however his mind is working right now, help him to feel grateful for his mind.

Thank you for Grandpa's mind.

When you see the time is right, could you let him see me giving him a hug—just so he knows that his mind is good and kind?

I ask this in your name...

February 19

God,

Did you know that my Grandpa is an amazing man? He has loved in ways that are truly amazing for human people (and he's a wonderful human people)!

Thank you for the many ways you lead Grandpa to express love, and thank you for the many ways you open people's hearts so his love can be felt and experienced.

Thank you for the amazing man that is my Grandpa.

Vibrantly...

February 20

For food, today, we are grateful, Dear Lord.

I'm grateful that Grandpa has good food to eat. You always provide for my Grandpa, and he never goes hungry.

As he nourishes his body with food and nutrients, nourish his soul so that he knows your wondrous and guiding love.

When his belly is full, help his heart to feel nourished as well.

Amen.

February 21

Brrrrrrrrrrr!

That cold wind feels like it goes straight through my bones today. When Grandpa feels cold, could you also help him feel something warm—in his heart, on his hands, wrapping his body to keep him warm.

Help him know this warmth is full of love from me to him.

Thank you, God.

February 22

Guiding Father,

Your always-present grace
watches over us all.

As you watch over Grandpa today,
help him remember to be thankful
for friends. Friends are grace-full.

Thank you for all the friends that
touch Grandpa's life.

Gracefully...

February 23

God of Life,

I'm feeling ordinary today. It's
good to have ordinary days.

I like the ordinary feeling of having
a Grandpa that loves me—and that
he has a Grandchild that loves him.

Thank you for what helps life
to seem ordinary.

Deliciously...

February 24

Oh, Dear God,

For family, we are grateful. Families give us opportunities to grow our hearts and our selves. We're fortunate to have the family we have. Thank you for the for the Grandpa I have in this family.

Thank you for right now!

February 25

Well God,

Time for some pillow talk. I love the comfy feeling of laying my head on a pillow at night. It cradles my head and signals a time for rest.

Well, I was wondering if you could help Grandpa know that comfy feeling today. Grandpa helps me to feel comfy about who and what I am.

Grandpa snuggles...

February 26

Dear God,

Something tells me Grandpa
could use your help today.

I don't know what goes on right now,
but Grandpa's heart could use a little
burst of your love and guidance.

When I see the stars tonight, I'll thank
each one for guarding and guiding us.

Sleeping with angels...

February 27

Heavenly Father and Creator,

I'm so glad it worked out for me to
have the Grandpa I have.

Thank you for your hand in making that happen.

In the creation of this day, thank you, too,
for creating blessings for us to discover.

Discovering blessings...

February 28

God,

Is two in one day too many? In years when we're leaping, is it okay to have two prayers for Grandpa in one day?

One prayer would be that Grandpa enjoys his nap today.

Another prayer would be that Grandpa smiles today.

February 29

Father in Heaven,

Leaping lizards, leaping years, and big giant leaps of faith. What are your thoughts about leaping? I'm taking a leap of faith that Grandpa will still love me when I share stories about myself with him.

Whatever Grandpa's leap of faith is, could you guide him with that today?

Leaping...

March 1

Wow God!

This year is marching right along!
(Pun intended.)

As Grandpa's year continues to unfold,
let his soul understand that our
souls love him dearly.

Help this year continue to
be full of blessings.

Thank you, Lord.

March 2

Good morning God!

Thanks for that bright, beaming sunshine you give us. It's good to know that your bright light is there, even when clouds color our skies.

When I see and feel this sunshine, I imagine that it reaches out and touches my Grandpa, and shines on his home, filling him with warmth and hope.

Adventurously...

March 3

Ouch! God!

My heart has an ouchy!
Does Grandpa's heart ever have any ouchies?

Sometimes life is not as gentle as I think it
should be. I know when my heart aches,
you're there, but sometimes I forget.

Ouchies often mean we're growing somehow.

When Grandpa has a heart ouchy, could
you shower him with awareness that he's
growing and that you're there to help?

Authentically...

March 4

Blessed Lord,

I feel angry sometimes. Is it possible that Grandpa feels angry too? After I feel angry and I calm myself down, I always find ways to learn from the angry feelings I have.

When Grandpa feels angry, could you enlighten him so he can learn about himself?

Thanks for the way anger can teach us about ourselves.

Stretching...

March 5

Dear Father in Heaven,

I want to talk about nightmares. Does Grandpa ever have startling dreams when he sleeps?

I know these dreams help our souls process whatever is going on in our lives. But they can be disconcerting sometimes.

If Grandpa has bad dreams, will you please touch him, so he knows everything will be okay?

Supportingly...

March 6

Heavenly Father,

Every day, we grow older. Grandpa has had more days in his life than I have. I don't know how he feels about getting older, but I know it can be scary sometimes.

Help Grandpa know that getting older is part of what it means to live life.

Help him see continued purpose in his life.

Thank you for the gifts of aging and the wisdom that happens!

March 7

Dear God,

My Grandpa is such an inspiring man. He inspires me.

Who inspires him? As he travels through this day, would you please inspire Grandpa?

Thank you for the ways you open my heart to be inspired by him.

Inspiringly...

March 8

Hey God,

I was wondering about something.
When I feel love for my Grandpa, can he feel that?

I believe I can feel it when he loves me.

When that happens, it's like the Grandpa pocket in my heart spills over and touches other parts of me.

Help Grandpa to feel it when I love him.

Curiously...

March 9

Mighty Father,

Sometimes I have days that just taste bad—
I just would rather that didn't happen.

When the bad-tasting day is over, and another
day happens, the day that tasted bad
invites my heart to grow.

When Grandpa has a day that doesn't taste so
great, can his heart be invited to grow, too?

Experimenting...

March 10

Hello God?

Are you there?
Are you really there? Where are you?

Life is always so full of change, and I know change is a blessing. But sometimes it's hard to remember that you're there.

If Grandpa is having trouble remembering that you're there, could you send him a gentle reminder?

Faithfully...

March 11

Dear God,

I noticed a bird soaring through your grand universe the other day. When I see a bird soaring, I'm reminded of how vast your universe is, and how small my part of it seems.

If there is a way for Grandpa to feel my love for him, vast like your universe, I'd like that for him.

Expressively...

March 12

Father above,

Just before the seasons change, I
notice a change is coming.

Maybe it's a day that feels like
spring or smells like spring—but
spring hasn't quite sprung yet.

As Grandpa's life changes, could
you give him a gentle nudge?

Let him know you're right
there in his heart.

Thank you.

March 13

Father of possibilities,

Does Grandpa still have dreams? I
know when he was younger, he had
dreams about the life he wanted.

I wonder if he still has dreams.

If he does, can you please point him in
the right direction so his
dreams can come true?

Daydreaming...

March 14

Gracious Father,

There is a miracle in my life today.
Grandpa knows that his Grand-ones journey
through life with him in their hearts.

It feels like a miracle that we can share in
life with each other. Whatever miracle Grandpa
might experience today, let it deepen and
enrich his life.

Miraculously...

March 15

God? It's one of your children,

Sometimes I have a day and I just feel crabby.
When I feel crabby, nothing seems to go right.

If Grandpa has a crabby day, could you help him
remember that you still love him even when
it's hard for him to remember that?

Thank you for loving Grandpa when he's crabby.

March 16

Father God,

Grandpa's life is like a treasure chest.

His stories are treasures. When I
discover new things about him, it's
like finding a genuine treasure.

Thank you for all the treasures that
come with this person I call Grandpa.

Passionately...

March 17

Fun one,

Is Grandpa wearing green?
We're celebrating green today.
Quick, Grandpa, find some green!
Don't get pinched!

I don't want anyone to pinch my Grandpa—quick,
help him find some green!

Little green men...

March 18

About tools, God...

Grandpas have lots of tools. My Grandpa is no
exception. His garage is full of all kinds of tools he
uses to fix things, to build things, to create holes in
things, to give something a fresh coat of paint.

When Grandpa needs just the right tool for
whatever requires attention, will you guide him
to the perfect solution for his needs?

Handy dandy...

March 19

Dear God,

Today I'm reflecting Grandpa's gentle side.

Any Grandpa, who is a Great-Grandpa, and allows himself to be called Grandpa Grape surely must be a gentle Grandpa.

Remember how gentle Grandpa is.

March 20

Dear Jesus,

Does Grandpa ever write letters to you? Letters to you don't have to be very long, just a line or two.

If Grandpa would like to write you a letter, maybe he could jot it down and put it under a pillow. Then, when he rests on that pillow, your angels will be there to take care of him.

Resting with Angels...

March 21

Guardian Lord,

I'm not sure what Grandpa has in store for his day today.

If he's traveling from one place to another, please provide him with traveling kindnesses.

Bless his travels so that he might know your presence.

Caring...

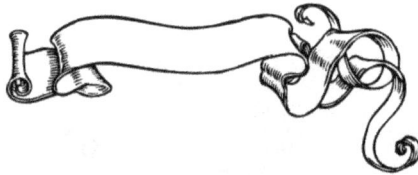

March 22

Just a minute God.

You are so patient and affectionate, God.

Sometimes we need an extra minute to take care of whatever life is happening at any given moment.

If Grandpa needs an extra minute for something today, help him know your gifts of patience and affection are with him.

Momentarily...

March 23

You know, God,

Grandpa has never had tons of money. But you know,
he always managed to have enough when he needed it.

Thank you for the wealth that you provide so that
Grandpa has what he needs, when he needs it.
(and a little extra for frivolous spending on occasion)

Thank you, Grand Provider.

March 24

Heavenly Father,

Once, when I was hurt,
Grandpa loved me anyway. That's
the way of your love.

If Grandpa is hurting, could
you let him know I love him?

Let him know the way
of your love.

Caring...

March 25

Dear God,

Does Grandpa really realize how important it is to be who he is? I'd like for him to know how important he is to me, and how important he is to everyone who knows him.

Grandpa is very important.

Grace-full-ly...

March 26

Wise and Wonderful Father,

Did you know Grandpa is an encyclopedia? He has his own brand of wisdom, because of his life experiences.

I enjoy learning from him. For Grandpa's wisdom and experience, I thank you.

Open...

March 27

Remember God?

Remember when I used to take a walk with
Grandpa after dinner? Well, his body
doesn't do those kinds of walks anymore,
but in my heart, I still walk with him.

Walk with Grandpa today, and let him
know that I'm walking with him too.

Step-by-step...

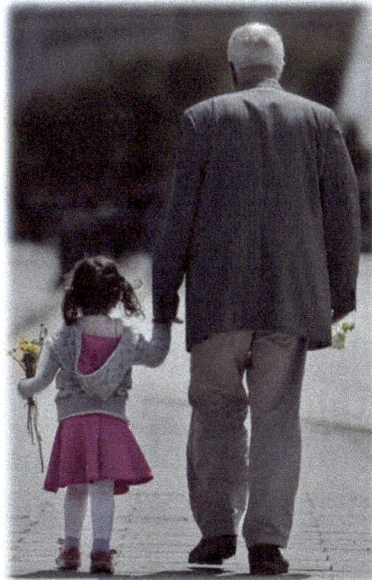

March 28

Gracious Father,

Thank you for giving Grandpa eyes to
see with. His eyes don't work as well as
they used to, but he can still see.

Especially, thank you for keeping the
eyes in his heart good and clear, so he
can see how much he is loved.

Abundantly...

March 29

Dear Lord,

That Grandpa is able to enjoy
something about today, I am grateful.
Thank you, too, for the pleasure
that comes with enjoyment.

Thank you for the pleasure of my Grandpa!

Amen.

March 30

Psssst! God!

Grandpa does have a tickle bone in him. He doesn't use it very often, but when he does, his whole body laughs and his eyes light up with life.

Would you be so kind and help Grandpa find something to get extra tickled about?

Thank you.

Playfully...

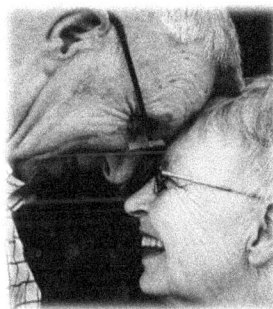

March 31

Good and Gracious God,

Goodness is surely one of your generous gifts.

Sharing my heart with Grandpa enriches
the goodness I feel with him.

I hope Grandpa feels goodness today.

Let his heart and soul overflow with goodness.

Sagaciously...

April 1

It's a little thing, God—

Ice cream is such a special treat. When I am aware of my Grandpa, like I am today, it's like a refreshing dish of ice cream.

Sweet thoughts are delicious moments for the soul. Thank you for this delicious moment.

Discovering...

April 2

God,

I know this is going to sound funny, but does Grandpa ever have a loose screw that needs tending?

We have so many tools to help us with our lives; Grandpas, screwdrivers, pausing for a moment of silence, and finding nice things to say to ourselves.

Whatever tool Grandpa is looking for, to fix something or to resolve something in his heart, could you please help him find what he needs?

Repairing...

April 3

Healing Father,

Is it possible that Grandpa could have
a day without pain today?

If pain is part of his journey, could you
help his heart understand what
the pain is teaching him?

Maybe it's physical pain, maybe it's a pain in
his soul, and maybe it's a pain of routine.

Help Grandpa to understand
more about his pain today.

Inquiringly...

April 4

Glorious and Mighty Father,

Grandpa is discovering something new today. I don't know what that is, or what it's about, but I suspect something new will settle into his consciousness today.

Thank you for new things; new days, new thoughts, new feelings, and new awareness.

Bless Grandpa with something new today.

Energetically...

April 5

Loving Lord,

Sometimes challenges come our way that we'd rather not deal with. If Grandpa has such a challenge in his life, could you help him know that the challenge is life-enriching?

Help him understand challenges can be blessings.

Reaching...

April 6

Awesome Father,

Sometimes we help people without ever being aware of it. Grandpa helped me the other day.

He shared some wisdom with me, and that reminded me of the treasure he is in my life.

He did not know the impact of his support, or how deeply he touches my heart.

Thank you for all the ways you help Grandpa, even when he is unaware.

Bless this angel unaware!

April 7

Lord, I gotta know something.

Does Grandpa still get any bubbly feelings on the inside because he's excited about something?

Does Grandpa still feel like clapping his hands and singing a happy song?

Does Grandpa still feel like the little boy that just got a new wagon for Christmas?

What do you think, Lord?

April 8

Hello God,

I was thinking about what it feels like after Thanksgiving dinner and we're all ready for a nap, just before the football game.

That is such a fulfilling experience—full tummies, family fellowship, time out to be aware of what we're thankful for. Anyway, could we wake up the feeling in Grandpa today?

Calm...

April 9

Lord,

Sometimes it seems that each day
is just the same old thing: the
same old routine; the same old
people; the same old food.

When Grandpa has a case of the
"same old stuff" could you throw
something in there so his "same
old world" is a little different?

Refreshingly...

April 10

Maybe he's in his chair resting. Maybe he's
reading a good book or the newspaper.

Perhaps he's just looking out the window,
wondering how his day will be. Maybe
he's aware that I love him and that he's
really special to me.

Whatever it is for Grandpa today,
thank you, Dear Lord.

April 11

God,

Sometimes it helps me to pick one thing and focus on that one thing until I get to a good stopping point. Then, I can think about another thing.

Does Grandpa ever feel that way? I bet he did, for sure, when he was younger. But does that still happen for him?

Whatever Grandpa's chaos is today, can you please guide him toward the right peaces to calm the storms?

Thoughtfully...

April 12

Creative Father,

Does Grandpa ever feel silly?
Silly is such a good feeling.

Here's something silly to think about. Imagine
what it would be like to be friends with a
talking toad. What sort of things would
you talk about? Gourmet bug snacks?

Maybe there's a way that Grandpa could feel
silly—in the kindest sort of way. Maybe when
he's silly, he can let a giggle come out.

Whimsical...

April 13

Sweet Jesus,

We've talked a little about family.
Thank you for the family we have and
our origin. Our family is deep and
rich with color-full lives and stories.

I'm glad I'm part of Grandpa's family now.

Thank you for Grandpa's
family—kinfolk and others!

April 14

Dear Lord,

...thank you for holding these prayers.

April 15

Dear Jesus,

Our government helps us sometimes.
I know it helps Grandpa.

I have the response letter he got from
President Roosevelt long ago. How amazing
that he reached out and got a response!

Sometimes, though, it seems the government is
not such a wonderful organization. On this day,
let us be thankful for our government
and the provisions therein.

Abundantly...

April 16

God of Wonder,

I see Grandpa's magic!
He's magic because he knows
how to bring people together.

Grandpa's magic because he
can make things out of wood.

He's magic because he's your child.

Magically...

April 17

Well, God—

The way it seems our life works, Grandpa has a
whole lot more years under his belt than I do.

If I get the pleasure of being a grandparent some
day, I hope I can contribute to my grandchildren's
lives the way Grandpa contributes to mine.

Giving...

April 18

Dear Lord,

Grandpa is extremely clever. He probably learned about this from his father, but he always has a pocket knife available to help open an envelope or a special package.

He always has his pocket knife available.

I think you, in some ways, are like a handy pocket knife for Grandpa. You're always there to help open things.

Creatively...

April 19

Nurturing Father,

Grandpa always has some apple butter handy
for toast. Isn't it interesting how we can
make so many things out of apples?

Apple sauce, apple pie, or just the apple,
the way it grows on trees.

You make interesting things out of Grandpas.

For the many ways you nurture us, I thank you.

April 20

Merciful Jesus,

There are lots of people in this world that
forget about their grandpas.

Every single day I enjoy knowing that I know
my Grandpa. I hope he feels like he's a person
deserving of respect and honor.

With enduring spirit...

April 21

First things first, God!

Grandpa is loved.
I love Grandpa.

Lots of people love Grandpa.

Hugs...

April 22

Surprise Father!

Life is full of surprises and undiscovered treasure.

Grandpa may be undiscovered to some folks,
but he is a hidden treasure to me.

Revealing...

April 23

Thanks, God!

Thank you for awareness.

Awareness helps us discern how we feel, what we understand about life, and what's going on around us.

I appreciate being aware of Grandpa.

That's all.

April 24

Whee God!

I was out in the spring rain yesterday and found a mud puddle. I took my shoes off and wiggled my toes in the mud.

What a great feeling, squishing mud between my toes! When was the last time Grandpa squished mud between his toes?

Dare he try it again someday?

Squishy mud!

April 25

Knowledgeable Lord,

You've deeply touched my Grandpa's heart
and you know all about him.

However, he needs to be touched today.

Open his heart so he can receive your blessings.

Thank you, Lord.

April 26

How much longer, God?

When will we get there?

How much longer do I have to endure?

Isn't it time yet?

Whatever Grandpa's question is
for him today, may enlightenment
be his blessing today.

Awakening...

April 27

Ever-Present God,

Is there a special friend in Grandpa's life—
someone he is remembering today?

Maybe it's a friend from his childhood.

Maybe it's a friend he had when he first got married.

Whoever his friend is, I hope these
are enriching thoughts for him.

Constantly...

April 28

Generous Father,

Does Grandpa ever ask you for forgiveness? If
he does, I hope you will respond abundantly.

Whatever Grandpa seeks forgiveness for, I
hope you can ignite his soul with blessing.

Setting it free...

April 29

Marvelous Father,

Today I walked in the
green grass barefoot.

It's a fresh and rejuvenating
thing to wiggle my toes
in your soft grass.

Does Grandpa ever wiggle
his toes in your grass?

Spritefully...

April 30

You know, God,

We've been having these daily chats for a good long
while now. I'm reminded of guest books.

When you touch our lives with gifts and blessings,
it's like having you sign the guest book of our life.

Thanks for signing Grandpa's guest book every day.

Presently...

May 1

Wow Jesus,

Let's talk about free spirits. What a joyous feeling that we can allow our spirits to be free.

If Grandpa is having a hard time with freeing part of his spirit, could you encourage him to make a choice to practice freedom?

Freely...

May 2

Hey God,

Splish splash!
When was the last time Grandpa made a big splash? Maybe he dropped the soap in the bathtub, or maybe he dropped some-thing into some dishwater.

It's fun to make big splashes in the swimming pool; I jump in with my whole self from the side of the pool.

I bet it's been a while since Grandpa jumped into a pool. Maybe you could help him make a big splash; dropping his spoon into some dishwater, or stomping hard in a small water puddle.

Exhilarating...

May 3

Father,

It seems like we have a place for everything.
We put our clothes in the closet or drawer.
We file away our feelings to 'explore them later.'

Everything has its place and there seems to be a
place for everything. But what happens when
we come across something new that doesn't
fit into a specifically defined box?

Sometimes what my heart needs is to explore
outside the box a little bit. If Grandpa could
use an out-side-the-box awareness today,
usher that awareness for him.

Marvelously...

May 4

Hello God,

I noticed the other day that my Grandpa is very courageous. He must get courage from you because it seems so unwavering. I want him to be aware of how inspiring his courage is for me.

Thank you for the gift of courage that you bless Grandpa with. When he requires courage, would you keep it strong for him?

Blessings...

May 5

Tell me, God.

When I read out loud to myself, I often internalize things differently than when I read silently to myself. When was the last time Grandpa read a book out loud?

Is there a little book that Grandpa could read out loud to himself today, or maybe part of a book?

When he reads to himself, I wonder if it is possible for him to hear himself and feel nurtured by that.

Studying...

May 6

God of life,

Does Grandpa remember the last
time I gave him a big hug?

Those are good things to remember.
Maybe he could put his right hand on his
left shoulder, and his left hand on his
right shoulder and squeeze.

There.

It's like I'm giving him a hug right now. I
hope he feels love coming from me to him.

If he doesn't get many hugs,
help him remember to hug himself.

Endearingly...

May 7

Good God,

Like desserts after a good meal, life has dessert moments, too. Spending time with Grandpa is like savoring a delicious dessert.

Flowers are desserts for our eyes. Candy corn, now that's a nice little dessert; and Grandpa always has candy corn in his jar!

Today I hope Grandpa gets a candy corn somewhere in his life—a nice little sweetness that soothes and encourages.

Respectfully...

May 8

God?

When Grandpa tells me stories about his
life, I feel enchanted. I often wonder how
Grandpa did things when he was growing up.

His stories help me understand that
everyone's journey is unique, but it also gives me
opportunities to learn from him, and about him.

It's enchanting.

Today when Grandpa reads this prayer, and
learns more about what's going on inside me,
I hope he feels enchanted.

Embrace...

May 9

Yes Lord!

Grandpa's listening...

May 10

Delightful and Kind Spirit,

I have a dream that someday I will touch a life.
Touching lives is like extending encouragement
and validation into the world.

I like to feel encouraged and validated. I bet
Grandpa likes to feel those things, too.

When Grandpa connects with us today,
could you please open his awareness.

Make him aware that I'm encouraging him.
Allow him to feel like his life has value.

Hope-full-ly...

May 11

Gracious Heavenly Father,

Being alive is a remarkable thing. I want to feel alive in my day-to-day existence. It feels vibrant and wonder-full.

I wonder if you could help Grandpa to feel alive today.

Help him feel glad that he is alive today.

Remarkably...

May 12

Dear Father,

What would we ever do without friends? Friends are bubbles of life that help us feel connected and acknowledged.

Thank you for all the friends in Grandpa's life. Sometimes Grandpa is just the friend I want and need. I suspect his friends feel the same way.

Thank you for Grandpa's friends.

May 13

Loving Father,

Occasionally there are days that feel like an exercise in endurance. Some things we endure without much thought, and other days feel like an exercise in survival.

Each day, we face things we choose to endure. Endurance is something we build and look for.

Whatever Grandpa might be enduring today, it is my prayer that he knows you're there with him.

Courageously...

May 14

But God...

Sometimes I feel like an orphan. I know there are people in my life that love and care for me.

But today it is hard for me to feel that compassion.

Open my soul so I know that when I am feeling orphaned, I'm aware of your presence.

Let Grandpa feel you, too.

Longing...

May 15

Kind Father,

Anger is a feeling that abruptly comes to the surface. Someone says something or does something (or doesn't do something) and anger wells up inside like Old Faithful.

Anger feels destructive and evil sometimes; yet other times it feels full of energy. I'm just sure that Grandpa feels angry sometimes.

When he does, please help him understand his choices, and help him use the energy of anger to grow his spirit.

Exasperation...

May 16

Caring Lord,

I imagine that when something inside me heals, it also heals something in Grandpa.

When Grandpa is healing, send an angel to be with him. May his healing also heal me.

Gently...

May 17

God of all Creation,

You created many interesting people in our world. Grandpa is interesting because he knows how to fix cars. One stray rumble or rattle and Grandpa can tell you just what's going on under the hood of a car.

I imagine you can tell what's going on with us as we rumble and rattle our way through life.

Would you take a moment to help Grandpa figure out one rattle in his spirit?

Listening...

May 18

Playful Christ,

Lightening bugs are amazing!
I saw one of your lightening bugs today.

What a marvelous inspiration. Beings
come into our lives unexpectedly and light
our way. It's like lightening bugs for our
hearts. Grandpa is a special kind of
lightening bug for me.

Keep sending beings along the way to meet
up with Grandpa. Grandpas need
lightening bugs too, you know.

Buzzing...

May 19

Well God,

I don't feel like doing it! The mood isn't with me on this one. I'd rather be doing something else.

When I procrastinate, I'm not aware of the wonders of completion. When Grandpa procrastinates, help him know that it's okay, and wake up the miracle of completion.

When the time is right...

May 20

So how are we doing, God?

Goodness gracious. Is it the middle of May already? Where did the first days of this month go? (and so quickly)

Even though it may seem that this day is flying by, I hope Grandpa sees a flower or a growing plant today, and remembers that he is on a journey that shapes and molds his life.

Awareness...

May 21

Lord and Savior,

Does Grandpa ever get so wrapped up in himself that he forgets there's lots of people around who can help him?

There are days when I need to be saved from myself.

When I listen, you send someone to help me get outside myself. When Grandpa needs to be saved from himself, be there for him, or send someone his way.

Illuminating...

May 22

Father God,

Today I light a candle.
May the light of that candle reach
all the way to Grandpa's heart
and fill him with love.

You know what a dancing candle
flame is like; that's what it feels
like to have Grandpa in my heart.

Glowing...

May 23

Hello God?

Are you there? Hello! It's one of your
children—are you there?

Hello. Is anybody home? God, are you
there? I know you're there somewhere!

When I get still and listen, I notice your
presence. You're always there!

When Grandpa needs you, let him
know that you're there.

Searching...

May 24

Warm God,

How many nights does Grandpa tuck himself
into bed at night? When my kids were
young, and I tucked them into bed at night,
I would always say, "Sleep with angels."

When Grandpa tucks himself in for a night
of rest, would you touch him as he lays his
head gently upon his pillow?

Help him sleep with angels.

Settling in...

May 25

God of joy?

What is it about balloons? When I see balloons, the kid in me comes alive.

Does Grandpa remember a day when there were lots of balloons?

Today I imagine Grandpa's life filled with brightly colored balloons—each one filled with a joy about his life.

Past, present, future...

May 26

Honorable, Heavenly Father,

Where Grandpa lives, they display flags for
Memorial Day. Grandpa always speaks with
respect for those who've served our country.

Raising a family seems like it is
part of serving your country, too.

For all those who made our country
what it is, we thank you!

Respectfully...

May 27

Help God!

Sometimes I am just fed up with my life.
Sometimes life feels like a struggle.

If Grandpa ever feels that way,
would you shower him with
kindness—like you do for me?

Awaiting a sprinkle...

May 28

Hey Father,

When Grandpa is thirsty, can you please
provide him with just the right thing
to quench his thirst?

You know how sometimes a soda is just
what your tastebuds are thirsty for?

Then when you drink that soda, it just
quenches a thirst that you longed for.

I hope you can provide something for
Grandpa that will quench his thirst just
right!

Expectantly...

May 29

I'm free, Lord!

I'm flying free!
If humans had wings, today I would fly!

Remember what Grandpa felt like when
he went down a slide in the park?

Maybe he felt free, like a soaring bird.

I hope Grandpa still feels that way sometimes.

Zooming...

May 30

Almighty Father,

I know you know this.

Grandpa told me he loves Grandma very much.

What a wonderful gift it is to share in
knowing just how much he loves her.

I imagine that when Grandpa dies,
he'll still love Grandma big much!

Wow!

May 31

Whimsical Father,

Grandpa likes to feed your birds. He's always got some birdseed tucked away so your little flying beings can drop in for a snack.

If he doesn't have any seeds, maybe Grandpa could take a couple of crackers outside and stomp them with his bare feet.

Then your birds would have something to eat, and Grandpa could do something ticklish and outrageous.

Plentifully...

June 1

Beautiful Savior,

It's that glorious time of year when things
are vibrant with color and sleeping plants
are getting all dressed up for summer.

As Grandpa wakes from his rest today,
may he know that he's growing in the
light of your guidance, and he's getting all
dressed up for the coming summer.

Vivaciously...

June 2

God,

When Grandpa goes to sleep at the end
of this day, Help him feel full-
filled about the day he lived today.

Fill his cottage with angels that
watch over him and his home.

Let the angels be full of life and safety.

Patiently...

June 3

Watchful God,

What is it like for you to watch us live our lives? Sometimes I like to watch lizards.

It's fun to watch lady bugs and birds, too. I'm tuning my inner TV to the thought channel.

Thought watching can be enlightening. What is Grandpa watching today?

Observing...

June 4

Watchful One,

I like surprises! (Pleasant surprises, that is.) Grandpa used to leave extra change in his chair cushions and in the couch.

When I went to see him, I always found surprises.

Could you take a moment to leave a little extra surprise for Grandpa to find today? A coin or candy corn, or maybe the answer to a prayer?

Surprise...

June 5

Gentle, caring Father,

Sometimes I forget things, or I get my dates
mixed up. I wonder if Grandpa ever does that.
I know it is frustrating when my thoughts are
not as clear as I'd like for them to be.

Would you hold Grandpa with tender
caring when that happens for him?
A little patience goes a long way.

Clear thoughts...

June 6

Jesus loves him, this I know;
for the Bible tells me so.

Grandpas, Grandkids one and all,
we are thankful for it all.

June 7

Refreshing Savior,

There's nothing in the world quite like a gentle summer shower. It seems like the earth appreciates a little spritzer now and then.

Maybe it's not raining today at Grandpa's house. The next time you give him a gentle summer sprinkle, let him know it's okay to step outside—without an umbrella.

He can pretend that I'm showering him with hugs and kisses. (He won't melt.)

Freshen up...

June 8

God,

Do you ever write letters? Letters are like little packages of grace and kindness. The best presents!

When the time is right, would you write a letter to Grandpa and share with him a glimpse of your generous grace?

Glimmering...

June 9

Hello God,

It's me. I had a thought about prayers. I think when we say prayers it's like a fresh coat of paint for the soul. You know, it keeps the soul in good working order.

Grandpa must have a special prayer he'd like to share with you today. Please listen with your amazing open heart.

Calmly...

June 10

Dear Holy God,

I have a prayer jar I use to
remember people who want a
special prayer now and then.

Today Grandpa is in my prayer jar.

God love Grandpa real good!

June 11

Good day God.

I'm feeling serene and peace-full today. I hope Grandpa is
starting out his day with a dose of calm and serenity.

Seems to me like sharing these special feelings
with the world could help create more peace.

Let's create bridges of peace and let serenity
spill over the edges and into the world.

Spilling peace...

June 12

Ominous Father,

I behold the ocean as if it is a powerful symphony—everything carefully orchestrated.

The sea creatures and plants live harmoniously. Sure, there are some dissonances, but isn't that part of what life is all about?

I'm orchestrating a symphony between Grandpa and me today. Awaken our big symphonic hearts to our connection, and the connections we have with others.

Symphonically...

June 13

Ooooops, God!

It's already the middle of June!
You know how we set some profound intentions
when the beginning of a year rolls around?

Then a string of days happen, and before you
know it, it's the middle of the year.

Every day is a new adventure.

As Grandpa remembers this is still a year in
progress, maybe he could be the start of
something new—like the freshness of a new year.

Awareness...

June 14

Oh, God!

I feel so foolish! When I got dressed this morning, I put my leg in the wrong pant leg.

I could have been frustrated, but I chose to laugh instead. Does Grandpa ever feel foolish about something he's said or done?

Your bountiful grace cradles me when I feel foolish. When Grandpa feels foolish, could you cradle him in your grace?

Wondering...

June 15

I surrender God!

I can't do this my myself. What does Grandpa need to surrender to you?

Help him hand it to you.

Offering...

June 16

Hurry, God!

Send Grandpa a messenger.

Here's the message:
You are resourceful.

Refreshingly...

June 17

Yes God?

I'm listening...

June 18

Jesus,

Where did I put that? I can't find it!

Where in the lilies of Texas did I put that thing?

Grandpa is looking for something.

Would you be so kind as to help him find it?
I know he'll say thank you.

Discovering...

June 19

Wise One,

S-t-r-e-t-c-h. You know how it feels to stretch your arms and legs after a good night of rest?

Waking up just before or as the sun lights the way for a new day. Stretching is an energizing and refreshing way to start my day.

Maybe Grandpa will take time to have a good stretch today. And when he does, could you fill his cells with life and spunk?

Eagerly...

June 20

Dear Creator,

You created Grandpa and
you created lightning bugs.

Your creations are a wonder!

Glimpses...

June 21

Dear Jesus,

Sometimes I just try too hard. Does Grandpa
ever try too hard? I'm all about trying again,
but sometimes it turns into an insurmountable
challenge. Maybe that's when we need
to step back and take a breath.

Help us relax and allow things to unfold when
we're trying too hard. Sometimes pause or
redirection is what we need.

Deep breath...

June 22

Great Navigator,

It's time for an adventure. I think adventure finds people sometimes. Other times, I think we need to look for it.

Adventure comes in all shapes and sizes. Maybe Grandpa is due for an adventure.

Maybe a trip to the hamburger store or maybe a trip to a hardware store for some window shopping. Perhaps his adventure is simply having a chat with a friend.

Happening...

June 23

Dear God,

I can always trust Grandpa to have an open heart when I see him.

No matter what the circumstances, I can always trust that Grandpa cares about me.

I can always trust that you walk with Grandpa through his life.

Trusting...

June 24

Caring Lord,

Sometimes people are unkind and I feel betrayed. Does Grandpa ever feel betrayed?

When he has these feelings, I hope he remembers you can help him with that.

Would you please help us understand?

Mending...

June 25

Can you hear him Jesus?

He's doing it quietly, but Grandpa is humming
a familiar tune. There's a song in his heart.
Is it okay if he sings out loud?

He can hear his song when he sings out loud.

Rejoicing...

June 26

Tender Lord,

Is Grandpa hiding something? Is there something he
just doesn't want to admit to? You know, Lord,
sometimes I don't want to admit to things—like
own up to my thoughts or actions. When I admit
to things, it helps me be honest with myself.

Even something simple like—I admit I could be
more patient with someone. I hope Grandpa
can be honest with himself today.

Willingly...

June 27

Father,

Grandpa is a gift from God.

He blesses my life with stories, his open heart, with his candy jar, with his love, with himself.

Thanks for Grandpa Gifts.

June 28

Yippee Jesus!

Grandpa won!
We played a game of Yahtzee
and Grandpa won.

I like it when Grandpa wins.

I hope he wins today.

Celebrate...

June 29

Astounding Savior,

I made an invention once. I've written prayers, and ways to fix things. When I made a choice to be who I am, I invented an interesting person.

What sort of things does Grandpa invent?

He made a fun backyard ride for his kids when he was a young father. As a preacher, he invented lots of sermons to help people learn about you.

What is Grandpa going to invent today?

Building...

June 30

This is Yours, God.

Grandpa is yours.
Thank you for sharing him with me.

All your people are special,
but when you made Grandpa,
you created a gift for me.

I'm glad he listens to you.

Sowing...

July 1

Over here, Lord.

I want to try something; something new. I'm going to whisper something I like about Grandpa and set it free upon a breeze.

Do you think you could carry my sentiments on that breeze all the way to his house? Could you make it so he feels it in his heart?

Whoosh...

July 2

Just a minute Lord.

You know, this relationship I have with my Grandpa has taken time. Each day it changes; every year we learn new things that change our lives.

I'm grateful for the time I've had to share with Grandpa, for that time has made us who we are today.

I'm grateful for the time we have yet to experience.

Timing...

July 3

Dear Father,

There's something liberating about giving myself an opportunity to be loud. A good scream or a boisterous laugh creates an energy like no other.

Can you hear me? I'm shouting at the top of lungs!

Did you hear me squeak out loud when I got a letter from Grandpa? It feels good to shout a little!

Does Grandpa ever shout to himself?!!
Quietly or out loud?

Do you think he could get in his car, drive out to the farm, and let out a shout?

I LOVE YOU GRANDPA!

July 4

God of our land,

Today is a day we recognize our country's independence. Surely Grandpa feels independent sometimes.

Thank you, Lord, for the integrity that comes from being independent; as a nation, as a community, and as a person.

As a patriot...

July 5

Hey God?

I wonder what it is like to die.
I know it is part of life.

How does Grandpa feel when he thinks of death;
his death or perhaps the death of a loved one?

I believe when someone dies you've given us a
time to cry, to have joy, to feel empty, to feel
fulfilled, to miss someone, and to celebrate the
life. If Grandpa needs some understanding,
please be there for him.

Puzzled...

July 6

Jesus, I want to ask you something.

It seems to me there are gifts in being unknown.
What are your thoughts?

Let's take Grandpa for example. He's relatively
unknown—he made a church, but it's not
something the world at large knows about.

It seems to me that one of the gifts of being
unknown is how a person might change the world.

I believe that the world is a better place because my
Grandpa takes the time in his life to let me be a part
of his life. Isn't that good for your world somehow?

Curiously...

July 7

Star light, star bright,
first star I see tonight.

Shine on Grandpa's face
and make his eyes sparkle.

He wished he may,
he wished he might.

Could Grandpa have his wish tonight?

July 8

Hey God,

Let's talk about intentions. I meant to do that;
to clean the kitchen and do laundry. I meant to
do it, and I did it! I just wonder what
Grandpa's intentions are for today.

Whatever he intends, I wonder if you could be
with him as he accomplishes his intentions.

Intentionally....

July 9

Christ Jesus,

Thank you for trees. I hugged a tree
today—thanking it for all it does for me.

It gives me shade, it makes green leaves in
the spring, and red leaves in autumn.

In the winter it sleeps patiently
until the earth warms once again.

Maybe Grandpa could hug his chair today.
His chair does so much for him.

Supportingly...

July 10

Dear Lord,

Does Grandpa ever feel like he needs to be wound up to get his day going?

Today when I was getting ready to go to work, I wasn't quite as motivated as I usually am.

If Grandpa needs something to help him get things going today, I would especially appreciate it if you'd help him out.

Varoom...

July 11

You there, Father God?

If Grandpa is tired from carrying heavy burdens, help him come your way so that can give him rest.

Humbly...

July 12

Here God!

Grandpa has a box.

This is where he keeps his worries.

Here's Grandpa's box—we're going to let
you take care of these things for him.

Patiently...

July 13

Wow God!

Today is someone's birthday.
What if it's my birthday today?
Do you know what my favorite birthday present is?

I'll tell you. It's the ability to love Grandpa.

Thank you for allowing me to have a Grandpa to love.

Reaching out...

July 14

Mighty One,

I've got to get that letter written.

Oh, and I need to be sure there's enough groceries for the week. I need to do this and that, and this, too.

There's too much! It's like a wild herd of wildebeests! Can you help me tame these beasts?

If Grandpa needs help with his beasts, would you help him too?

Out of control...

July 15

Blessed Savior,

You know my Grandpa?
He sometimes wonders about my
choices, but he's generally confident in me.

Is it possible that he has a day when
he doesn't feel so confident?

It's a fancy thing that you always
provide confidence when I ask
(sometimes even when I don't ask).

Maybe if Grandpa wants some confidence,
you could give him a little boost.

Accomplishing...

July 16

Ahhhhh Father,

Shower Grandpa with different graces today.

(Here's an umbrella if you need one.)

July 17

Constant Lord,

Sometimes Grandpa cries. I hope he gives
himself permission to cry when he needs to.

Tears have a way of helping us see things more clearly.

When Grandpa cries, please wipe his tears and
let him know you're there with him.

Comfort...

July 18

Ummmm, God?

Did you see Grandpa's beautiful yard? He is so attentive to keeping his yard all trimmed and mowed. He does all sorts of things, behind the scenes, to be sure our lives are full of beauty and wonder. It would be so nice if you could do something behind the scenes for Grandpa today.

Tending...

July 19

God,

I can't seem to figure this out! Will I ever get it?

I try this; I try that, and nothing works!
Is Grandpa ever discouraged?

When I'm discouraged, Grandpa
knows just the right thing to say.

If I could say the right thing to him,
bless my lips for him.

Meaning...

July 20

It's party time, Jesus.

Bring out the party hats, the noisemakers, and
let's get a special cake for the occasion.
What are we celebrating?

I'll tell you what we're celebrating.

We're celebrating Grandpa's house. We're
celebrating his life. Let's celebrate Grandpa's
marriage and his haircuts and his mind.

Celebrate with Grandpa—
whatever he wants to celebrate.

Praising...

July 21

Hi God.

Let's chat about Grandpa's lap. I wonder how many hours of my life I spent in Grandpa's lap.

How nurturing. How loving.

Perhaps you could let Grandpa sit in your lap. I bet he could use some nurturing and love.

Reciprocating...

July 22

Steady Savior,

What does Grandpa believe in? I believe in goodness; truth and I believe in you.

I believe in Grandpa; he's one of your children, too. Oh, I believe in myself and my family.

I believe in writing, and I believe in song. I believe you're with him, and Grandpa believes in you, too.

Faithfully...

July 23

Summer Son,

It feels good to go outside and feel
your sunshine on my skin.

When Grandpa goes someplace today and he feels
your warm sun on his Grandpa self, maybe he'll
think it's me reaching down to give him a hug.

Toasty warm...

July 24

God?

I walked with a friend who is recovering
from back surgery. He is so inspiring.

Every day he walks a few more steps.
Does anyone ever walk with Grandpa?

Maybe they walk with him to the door or
around the block. Wherever Grandpa walks
today, will you please walk with him?

Journeying...

July 25

Time for a pow-wow, God.

Can we talk for a few moments?
Sometimes Grandpa forgets.

It must be hard for him when he can't remember.
I hope Grandpa remembers how much I love him.

Even if he can't remember that, maybe he can feel it.

Remind him, now and then, how much I care
about him; how much you care about him.

What do you think?

July 26

Anointing Lord,

I dropped an ice cube in my glass and it made a
plunky sound as it splashed in my glass. Does
Grandpa ever giggle when something splashes?

When Grandpa takes a bath, does he ever splash just for
fun? Maybe Grandpa could have a good splash today.

Make it fun and let him know it's okay to giggle.

Splashes...

July 27

Good and gracious Lord,

Today I'd like to chat about meditating.
Meditating is a great way to learn, to listen.
It creates community when done with
others. Meditating alone opens soul
to be aware of new things.

In my heart today,
I'm meditating with Grandpa.

Soul searching...

July 28

Hi Father.

Some days feel like they creep by at a snail's pace.
Other days whiz by so fast I hardly notice.
Life offers us different tempos,
and I'm grateful for that.

I celebrate that we have variety in that
tempo from day to day. I was wondering
about Grandpa's tempo today.

What is his tempo?
Make it a tempo that helps him
and make it just right.

Infinitely...

July 29

How about it, God?

Playtime for Grandpa.

When was the last time Grandpa had some play time?

Maybe playing gardener or playing preacher.

Maybe he could play a game of Dominoes with a friend.

Frolicking...

July 30

Prrrrrecious One,

Someone just gave me a little back rub. Oh, that feels so refreshing and calming. When was the last time someone rubbed Grandpa's shoulders for a moment? I want to do that for him today.

I bet it would make him purr. Grandpa, can you pretend that I'm there with you in your living room, and I'm giving him a back rub?

Feel my warm hands as they nurture you?
(I think I can hear him purring!)

Ahhhhhh...

July 31

Loving Father,

I'm making up a holiday for today. I officially declare it Hug Awareness day.

As Grandpa journeys through his day, help him be aware of the many ways people hug him.

Help him be aware when he goes to church, when I see him, or when he gets to go out for ice cream, he gets hugs.

Ice cream is a hug for bellies.

Hugs and kisses...

August 1

Whew, God!

I wonder what Grandpa dreams about when he sleeps.

He may or may not remember his dreams; sometimes I don't. Maybe he remembers a dream he has—maybe not a night dream, but a daydream.

You know, like—I'd like to ride in a race car. Bless his dream. Take care of Grandpa's dreams so it is best for him.

Astonishingly...

August 2

Great teaching One,

Grandpa has lots of books in his house. Does he have any book friends? You know, books that comfort or books that touch his soul.

The Bible is one of my book friends. Help Grandpa find the perfect book friend today.

Preparing...

August 3

Psssst! Jesus!

Grandpa has a guest book at his house. Every time I go to visit him, I sign his guest book. When he reads the pages, he thinks about all the people who came to see him.

Here's an idea. Maybe Grandpa could sign his guest book on your behalf. He will remember you came to visit, too.

Autographs...

August 4

Dear Lord,

I wonder what it is like for Grandpa to see babies. He's getting in up years, and I wonder about his perspective when he sees babies.

I think about the wild adventure ahead for them, and hold them in my heart. I bet that's what it is like for you to look in on us.

When you see Grandpa, would you send him love and acceptance for me?

Changing...

August 5

Powerful God,

Grandpa is such a man of strength.
How did he manage in the 1930s when his wife
died, and he had two children under the age of three?

He must have a will and strength that comes from
you. Where did that strength come from when he
moved from his familiar house to an apartment?

If he's looking for strength, please provide
him with all that he needs.

Sturdy...

August 6

Lord Jesus,

You know what the Upper Room is?
Do we have upper rooms in our souls?
What do we keep in our upper rooms?

Is it the attic where we store stuff?
Maybe it's an intimate place where we
gather with ourselves in your midst?

Is it a place where we go when we're
looking for solace?

What is Grandpa's upper room?

Pondering...

August 7

Joyous Savior,

I wanted you to know that I enjoy my life. What does Grandpa enjoy? Does he enjoy the nature around him? Maybe he enjoys a good book, a conversation with a friend, or maybe even his walker (he calls it his dance partner).

Does he enjoy spending time with Grandma? Does he enjoy himself?

In joy...

August 8

Poetic Father,

I noticed something about a particular word—Expressive.

Pull it apart a little and you have ex-press. If you ex-press something, do you let it go or set it free? What are some things that Grandpa wants to express?

He expresses he cares; that he is concerned. Allow him to express from his heart.

Eloquently...

August 9

God,

Grandpa's life is like a good book.
I keep wanting to turn the page to learn more about
what happens. This book has many varied chapters.

When he starts his day, he begins a new portion of
the book. This book has many tones and melodies.

If you read carefully, there are goodies
that appear between the lines.

I like the book called Grandpa.

Absorbing...

August 10

(To the tune of Lead On O King Eternal)

Lead on, Grandpa I'm watching. You have a solid path.

Please let me walk beside you, as I enjoy your hand.

Remember that I love you, remember that I care!

Whenever you are lonely, remember God is there.

August 11

Courageous God,

When was the last time Grandpa tried something new? I'm trying something new today. When I look at my hands, I see Grandpa cradled there.

Would you give him a gentle nudge and let Grandpa know it's okay to try something new today? Try doing something different; try changing the order of your day.

Maybe try a new food. Try, try, try, try, try.

Guarding...

August 12

Father,

Grandpa is a grandpa because he's older than me.
Older means aging. What does aging mean?

When Grandpa ages, how does his perspective
change? Do unknown parts of him awaken?
What does Grandpa think about aging?

When aging happens, does he accept that
he's an old person? Old people are blessings;
I know Grandpa is a blessing to me.
Walk with Grandpa as he ages.

Maturing...

August 13

Lord,

I was wondering about something. As we go through our lives, we have dreams we want to come true.

What does Grandpa dream about for his life?

What does he want for his life, going forward?
Do we ever get to the end of those dreams?

It seems to me that when we attain a goal or reach 'those points' in our lives, dreams then change and we just keep on striving.

How does that work?

Curious...

August 14

Wondrous One,

Let's visit about tenderness.
Boo-boos require tenderness, kitties require
it, and tenderness is for people, too.

I think Grandpa needs tenderness sometimes.
Grandpa is always tender with me and I
desire to share the same with him.

Help him receive tenderness and be tender
for himself whenever it's meant to be.

Softly...

August 15

Wait God!

What time is it? Can I get just a little more time?
Sometimes time is an impatient deadline.
Other times, though, time can be so
healing and requires savoring.

What time is it for Grandpa?
If he needs time, would you grant it to him?

If it's time to get moving, will you give him a nudge?

Tick tock...

August 16

Yikes God!

It feels like it's time to be a little crazy. Is it okay for Grandpa to be a little crazy, too? We can do silly things together. What would happen if Grandpa ate ice cream with a fork?

How about putting a squeeze of a fresh orange slice in his bath water? Let's eat dessert first today.

Could he wash his hands with milk or sprinkle cinnamon in his coffee?

Wild things...

August 17

He caught one, Lord!

Grandpa likes to go fishing. I know he taught my dad how to fish and he still enjoys doing that today. It is one thing to fish for a meal and quite another to fish for solutions to challenging things. Whatever Grandpa is fishing for, perhaps you could guide him along the way.

Patiently...

August 18

Spiritual Father,

Remember years back when Grandpa and Grandma married? When his first wife died, he got married again, and now she's my Grandma. The only Grandma I've ever known.

There must be many lessons in Grandpa's life he learned by being married. Thank you for teaching him—thank you for helping Grandpa learn.

Loving...

August 19

Yummy God,

I love eating cold grapes out of the refrigerator in the summer. Does Grandpa have any grapes? How many grapes can he put in his mouth at once?

I think I can get 13 grapes in my mouth. Sometimes I put too many in my mouth and grape juice squirts out on the table.

Now that Grandpa lives by himself, you think he might try playing with grapes?

Frivolous...

August 20

Happy Father,

I'm feeling like giving Grandpa a gift today.
I was wondering if you could stir a memory in my Grandpa's heart and let the memory be a gift for his soul.

Stir a memory that's just right for him today.
Maybe a memory about something funny
he heard his Daddy or Mommy say.

Astonishingly...

August 21

Great Navigator One,

Thank you for guiding us as we travel.
We go places with our hearts, our cars, our
souls, our minds, and our feet.

Which way do we go?
How do we decide where to go?

Sometimes it's hard for me to know the correct
decision, or which decision is best for all
involved. When I decide, there is
freedom; it allows us to move on.

Miraculously, the life that happens because of a
choice unfolds golden opportunities.

Thank you for helping us travel.

August 22

Okay God!

Did you know that Grandpa's last officiating engagement as a pastor was to facilitate the presentation of rings at my wedding?

What an honor to have him be a part of that momentous occasion. I bet Grandpa served many people as a pastor.

He married them, buried them, & gave them food for their souls.

An amazing servant, that one!

Please help Grandpa to feel the honor that so many people, such as myself, feel for him.
He is a dear servant.

Thank you for Grandpa and his gifts...

August 23

Yodle-le-hee-hoo Lord!

It's true.
Grandpa is a giant!
He is a quiet giant.

He has a heart bigger than the state of Texas
and his soul is deeper than the ocean.

He goes about his existence each day, taking
on the challenges that face him, and he just
keeps on keeping on—steady as he goes.

He is a quiet giant, and he blesses my life richly.

Can he hear me?...

August 24

Ha ha ha Father.

I can't seem to stop laughing! This just started being a little chuckle, then it turned into a giggle.

From there I lost control and now I'm laughing so hard I have tears in my ears!

Heeee, heeee, ha, ha, heeee, heee!

Grandpa has a great chuckle, and I love it when he laughs himself into a full-on belly laugh.

Help Grandpa find something fun to laugh about today. Tell him it's okay to laugh out loud!

Grinning...

August 25

Hello, God!

It's hot out here today! Thank you for warmth, and thank you for allowing it to cool off and not be so hot all the time.

I bet Grandpa is hot today, too. What can he do to cool down? What will be refreshing? A splash of cool water on his face?

An air conditioner? A cool bath? A blessing from you?

Whoooosh!...

August 26

Well God,

My Grandpa can be serious sometimes. There is a time and place for that, for sure. I wonder, though, if he could do something outrageous, just for fun today.

Maybe he could play with some jello. Perhaps he could create a mountain out of his mashed potatoes.

I bet he could make a paper airplane out of his newspaper! Would it be okay for Grandpa to play today?

Outrageously...

August 27

There you are, God.

I see you dancing! You're in the playful waves in the swimming pool and in the rush of people going to the store to pick up groceries. When Grandpa gets himself a snack, I see you dancing a dance of nourishment.

Do you suppose he could, even now, play some gentle music and dance a gentle dance? He can even wiggle a little dance in his chair if he chose to.

I imagine that if he danced, he would smile from the inside out! And, so would you!

Wheeeee!

August 28

Look here God!...

Thank you for what you showed me today.
It's good to open my eyes to new possibilities.

What does Grandpa see? What does he visualize his ideal day to be? When he thinks of the coming autumn, what does he see?

Sensing...

August 29

God,

I know I ask a lot of questions. I ask questions because I'm curious, because I want direction, because I want to uncover the miracle of the moment.

Asking is something I sometimes forget to do though, because I just want to take care of things on my own.

When Grandpa needs or wants something from someone, whether it's you or another friend, would you help him to feel free to ask?

Exploring...

August 30

Jazzy Jesus,

When I do laundry, I sometimes pretend you're washing my soul. I wash clothes; you wash souls.

When I dried my clothes, I let some sunshine into the fabric of my soul. While folding clothes, I found a place for one of my cares and worries.

When I put my clothes away, I handed my heart to you. (Grandpa does laundry, too, you already know!)

Reverently...

August 31

Amazing Father,

Is this the last day of August already?
There won't be any more days in this August this year.

Make today something special for Grandpa.

Maybe he'll remember it's his great-grand-son's birthday today.

Open his heart to something special today.

Gratefully...

September 1

Loving Father,

Let's talk about smiles. We have warm smiles, silly ones, giggly ones, and growing ones.

Different smiles are full of different stories. What is Grandpa smiling about today?

What story does his smile tell? When he smiles today, please help him connect with the story behind his smile.

Grinning...

September 2

Just in time Father...

You know when Grandpa needs a bolt or a screw to fix something, he always goes out to his workshop to find what he needs. Sometimes he goes to your house to find what he needs.

Thank you for being available in Grandpa's workshop.

Perfect...

September 3

It's time for a celebration, God!

Gifts come in all shapes and sizes. Today, though, I'm especially tuned into a very special gift—Grandpa.

Did you know, when you made him, that he would one day be my Grandpa? He is a special gift to me, and I know he is a special gift to other people too.

With the caring love you used when you created him, may that same caring love help him know that he is one of your wonderful children—a special gift.

You created a special gift—Grandpa.

September 4

Uhm, Lord?

You know what I'm hungry for? I'd like a big scoop of ice cream and a soft, gooey chocolate chip cookie. Just sounds good!

What is Grandpa hungry for today? It's my desire that whatever Grandpa's hunger is, you could present an opportunity for him to quench his hunger.

Satisfying...

September 5

Oh, Wise One,

You inspire me. Grandpa inspires me. He inspires me to walk sure and steady with my heart as a guide.

What inspires Grandpa?
What stirs the spark inside him?
When he is inspired, how does he feel?

What sparks his imagination?
What's inspiring Grandpa today?

Intriguingly...

September 6

Yes Lord Jesus?

...I see...

September 7

Happy Father,

I feel that today. There is a hint of fall in the air that tells me a change is coming. I like how you give us glimpses of changing seasons. It creates hope for new things on the horizon.

Did Grandpa catch a glimpse of something that brings him hope today? I wonder if you could create a glimpse of something delightful for Grandpa today.

What does Grandpa want or need that brings him hope?

Astonishingly...

September 8

Oh Dear God,

Sometimes it is difficult for me to let go of things in the past and get on with the here and now. I have an idea.

Write a secret that's ready to be set free, and throw it away, or take the secret to you in communion and let you handle it in the mastery that is uniquely yours.

If Grandpa has something he'd like to set free, let him know of your presence. Guide him gently and invite him to let go.

Releasing...

September 9

Bravo Dear Savior!

Grandpa must be clapping his hands. What is he applauding? Is he clapping because he's singing a song and keeping time?

Maybe he's clapping because he appreciates someone or something someone has done.

Is he clapping because he wants to hear that sound? Is he clapping just because he feels like doing it?

Embracing...

September 10

Father God,

When you look into Grandpa's eyes, what do you see? Have you seen the sparkling twinkle in his eyes that never dims? I'm pretty sure that's his guiding light.

Have you noticed the enriching green and blue that surrounds him? He must be part of your rainbows. I like how Grandpa feels down in his soul. It's like a glowing radiation that embraces and guides.

Splendor...

September 11

Caring Lord,

When we have caring people in our lives, it's like having a deep well of caring resources at our fingertips.

I don't know exactly how it works, but caring helps me feel seen and understood somehow.

I hope Grandpa has a full well of people who care for him. Can you please help him be aware of the caring that is all around him today?

Tremendously...

September 12

Wake Up Lord!

I mowed the grass in my backyard this morning. I wonder how many times Grandpa has done that in his life. Grooming our yards is like clearing a space for more things to grow. I hope Grandpa has lots of space in his heart for things to grow.

I hope he's growing a bumper crop of goodness in his heart.

Whirling...

September 13

Articulate Father,

You speak to us in many languages. Some languages are easier to understand than others. Do you suppose things like despair, depression, or anger are part of your languages? I think they are.

When I examine these feelings, something good is revealed—something that makes me grow.

Whatever language Grandpa is speaking or hearing today, help him understand.

Glowing...

September 14

I saw that, God!

I saw that when you made the leaves dance in the pre-autumn breeze. One of them looked like a graceful ballerina as it let go of the branch it has clung to all summer.

I saw that when you cooled the warm summer air to a brisk autumn air, even if only for a few early morning moments.

I saw that when you wrapped your arms around Grandpa's life and held him.

Peeking...

September 15

Working Father,

It seems like we spend a good part of our lives working. A good bit of that is job related, but we also work on our homes, our families, and growing ourselves into who we are meant to be.

You are always working, too. I say that because you're available to us, any moment of any day or night.

Help Grandpa to know that I'm thankful, to know that his love is always there for me.

Surely...

September 16

God of Grace,

Did you ever make a mistake? I made one today. I learned something, though, because I made that mistake.

Does Grandpa ever make mistakes? I bet he's made one or two. It's part of what makes us human. It doesn't always feel good, but it's interesting how much we learn if we choose to pay attention. When Grandpa does a mistake, I hope you're there to teach just the right lesson.

Grace-Full...

September 17

Faithful Savior,

I see my Grandpa as one of your faithful servants. He touches lives because you made him who he is. Grandpa helps me live life.

He prays for me and he loves me with his heart of gold. He asks for your guidance and he reads about you.

I just want to say thank you for being faithful to him.

Contentedly...

September 18

Plentiful God,

Sometimes there seems to be more
month than there is money. Has
Grandpa ever felt that way? Does he ever
wonder if there is going to be enough?

Does Grandpa have enough?
Will there be enough for Grandpa?

Thank you for always supplying what is
needed. I hope Grandpa has enough for
today and all the coming days.

Abundantly...

September 19

Dear Father,

Nothing is right today. Nothing is working right.
Everything I try to do just doesn't work out the
way I'm intending for it to. It doesn't feel good,
and life is just hard today.

Does Grandpa ever feel this way? I think he does
because he is one of your children. If something
isn't right for Grandpa, help him through that.
Help him embrace what is hard and help him learn.

Seeking...

September 20

Stable and Steady Father,

When I walk a narrow path in the mountains, up high, I don't always feel stable or steady. Does Grandpa ever feel unstable?

When I feel that way, fear comes by for a visit. I'm afraid I'm going to fall off the side and go tumbling.

If Grandpa is looking for some stability, would you please reassure him that sure and steadiness is already his? I want Grandpa to feel safe and stable.

Tranquilly...

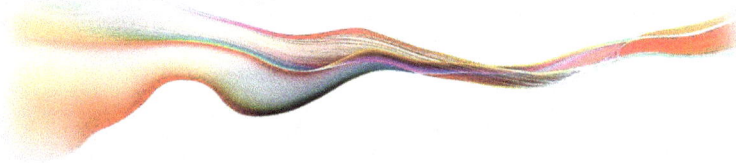

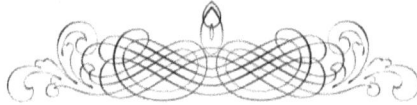

September 21

What do you think, Lord?
What are your impressions of Grandpa?

My impression of Grandpa is that
sometimes he feels afraid.

I think he feels great to be alive sometimes.

Sometimes Grandpa feels like peanut
brittle and other times he feels like a
cuddly teddy bear.

Impressions...

September 22

Over here, God!

I got in trouble today. I made a choice that seemed like
the right one, but someone scolded me for my actions.

My belly felt like a child who got a spankin'!

Does Grandpa ever feel that way? I guess we have
that feeling because it's time to be aware
of something important.

If Grandpa feels scolded, grant him the
awareness about what is important.

Troubled...

September 23

Enthusiastic Spirit,

Let's play a game. It's called Let the Book Speak.
Grandpa and I are going to take a book and
allow it to open to the page it wants to open to.

Then we're going to read a bit from the book
and let the words touch our lives today.

Boldly...

September 24

God! God! God!

Congratulations are in order!
Grandpa did it! I don't know specifically
what he's accomplished, but he
accomplished something.

Did you give him a "Job Well Done?"

Did you pat him on the back?
Did you tell him he's wonderful?

Ecstatically...

September 25

It's so good to be home, God.

Home is sometimes a refuge. It's a place where we do a large amount of living. When I come home from work, or a trip, home just feels good. It feels like an old friend.

It smells like home, and it somehow feels like a safety net. I'd like it if Grandpa could feel that feeling today and that he could feel good about being where he is.

Be calmed...

September 26

Super Duper Father,

Grandpa and I are doing something fun today, and you can play with us. We're going to look in the mirror, look into our eyes, and name something we're proud of about ourselves. Then we'll say thank you to you, for helping us be who we are.

Great game, huh?

Playing...

September 27

Fabulous Father,

When was the last time Grandpa made a new friend? Maybe he could be friends with his mail carrier, or with someone who helps him.

Sometimes I make friends with new feelings I'm learning about. It helps me understand what they want for me.

Sometimes old friends become like new friends when I discover new things about them.

I hope Grandpa still makes new friends. Maybe some of his new friends could be feelings.

Superbly...

September 28

God, alive and living,

Where are Grandpa's feet taking him today?
Is his path rocky or smooth? Wherever he
might be, whatever he might be doing, maybe
he will just have a good ol' day today.

Presently...

September 29

Truth or Dare?

Dare ya! I dare you, Grandpa,
to let me love you more.
I dare ya! Dare ya, Dare ya!

I could use a hug today;
that's the truth.

Maybe Grandpa is sending
me a hug right now!

Leaping...

September 30

Wondrous and Wise Creator,

Let's chat about this concept of things that last forever. Lives don't last forever, but your care and guidance does.

People in their human form don't last forever, but your love does.

Grandpa is important to me, but his body won't last forever. Won't the spirit of him last forever, though?

As long as I choose to keep it alive?

I believe Grandpa will always be with me—Grandpa angels are the best!

That's my story and I'm sticking to it!

Salubriously...

October 1

Fantastic Father,

What moves Grandpa to tears? Does he ever let himself cry when something meaningful happens?

Today I read a book and tears fell upon my face. Sometimes I watch movies and I let tears sprinkle my lap or pillow.

Why is our first instinct to make ourselves stop crying? These are good growing tears. Let them flow! When Grandpa feels like crying, I hope he will.

Strengthening...

October 2

Great God,

The world feels different when teachers and students return to the routine of school. The heartbeat of the world feels different to me. Has Grandpa ever noticed that? What's it like for him when it's school-time again? I hope Grandpa is still learning.

Inquisitively...

October 3

Just for fun, God,

Let's have a piece of cake with Grandpa today. I'm going to go to the store and find one piece of cake to enjoy.

When I eat it, I'm going to get two forks: one for my left hand and one for my right hand. I'll take turns, one bite for me, and one for Grandpa. I might even use my fingers to eat my cake. Then, I can lick off the icing when I'm finished.

Did Grandpa enjoy that moist cake and chocolate icing? (I did!)

Wild and free...

October 4

Jumpin' Junipers, Jesus!

What's the big rush? Hurry, hurry, hurry.

Sometimes hurry is the pace set for the day,
and it seems like there's just not enough
hours in the day to get it all done.

Stop! Take a breath! It's going to be okay!

When Grandpa feels rushed, I wonder if you
could help him realize what's most important?

The rest will wait.

Exhaling...

October 5

Nurturing Savior,

How are Grandpa's eyes today? Do they feel rested? Do they feel tired or scratchy? Are they sparkling with spunk and get-up-and-go?

One of my eyes is feeling stressed today; I think I have a stye (or something). I know you're tending to that, though.

Thank you! Whatever the way of Grandpa's eyes today, thank you for his eyes.

I'm glad he can see.

Luminously...

October 6

Father,

One of Grandpa's happy things is going to Meade for a hamburger. His little taste buds are happy when they wake up to that burger taste—juicy pickles, lettuce, a fresh tomato, a splash of mustard and maybe a creamy piece of cheese.

Sometimes hamburgers are just what Grandpa's tummy wants. Mmmmm. Think I'll have a burger, too!

Thank you for hamburgers.

October 7

Alright then, God.

Time for some one-on-one time with you. When Grandpa feels like it, could you talk with him about personal things while he listens to music?

Sometimes music helps our hearts to hear. He can pick out something that he likes to listen to, turn it on, lay down or sit comfortably in his chair.

Then he can close his eyes and let the music open the doors in his soul. Then you can touch his heart in just the perfect way.

Thank you for listening to Grandpa,
and for letting him share.

Treasure hunting...

October 8

Hear this prayer, Oh Lord,

Understanding is something that's difficult to find occasionally. Sometimes understanding hides from my awareness. Then there are times I feel like others don't understand me.

Is Grandpa looking for understanding? Does he want to be understood? Or is he looking to understand someone else? I found some understanding in my kitchen cabinet today.

Would you be sure Grandpa gets as much understanding as he needs?

Sharing...

October 9

Dear Holy Spirit,

There are days when Grandpa seeks solitude. I get that. Sometimes a good dose of solitude is just what I need. No outside noise or distractions. Just me and my thoughts. Solitude is good for us now and then. It's okay to ask for it and it's okay to create it.

When Grandpa seeks solitude, provide him with exactly what he's looking for.

Deep breath...

October 10

Hey God,

You know how we are always welcoming newborn babies into our world? I'm thinking that we need to welcome old born babies too—old born babies like grandpas and grandmas.

Grandpa, you are deeply wanted. Grandpa, welcome to our world. Grandpa, thank you for being here.

Pampering...

October 11

Constant Sprit,

Sometimes I take mini vacations in my mind, without ever getting in the car. Other times, I really go somewhere.

I always enjoy going to see Grandpa. Once, we took him to the place where he grew up, so we could hear his stories. (Grandpa stories are the best!)

Thank you for Grandpa's memories about vacations. Thank you for the vacation times he has in his mind.

Invigorating...

October 12

Gracious Father,

I got a letter in the mail today—to me, from me.
Did Grandpa ever write a letter to himself and send
it? I wonder if he would give himself such a gift.

He could write himself a love letter and write
about all the things he likes about himself.

He could even say "I love you" to himself.

Maybe he could write a memory letter and
write down memories to rediscover
when his package comes in the mail.

Insightfully...

October 13

Hey God,

Does Grandpa have any of that yummy hot chocolate? I'd like to be with him sipping on a mug of hot chocolate.

I know he enjoys his coffee. Maybe today he'd change it up so we can share some hot cocoa.

We're talking about what's going on in our lives—how people are doing and what's going on in the world.

Fellowship...

October 14

Embracing Father,

I think Grandpa's days are relatively quiet. Does he ever want to make some noise? How could he make some noise today? Maybe he could just say one or two words really loud.

"I'm here!" "My Grandchildren love me!" (Okay, that's more than two words, but that's okay.)

I'd love to see Grandpa make some noise.

Energetically...

October 15

Help! Jesus! Help!

Save me from myself! I can be soooo hard on myself sometimes. Is Grandpa ever hard on himself? Maybe he says things to himself that aren't very loving or understanding.

Boy! I'm pretty good at doing that myself. Would you lend Grandpa a hand when he's being hard on himself?

Asking...

October 16

(Another song, to the tune of Three Blind Mice)
Grandpa cares. He is fair.
See how he loves? O how he loves!
He goes to bed and he rests his head.
He loves his wife and is full of life.
He reads good books and he fixes the shelf.
Grandpa sneezed. A tissue please!

October 17

Everlasting Spirit,

Does Grandpa remember having stories read to him as a child? Today, I read a chapter of one of my favorite books out loud. I sat down in my chair, and read to myself.

I learn things when I read out loud to myself.

Maybe Grandpa could read out loud to himself someday. Read yourself a story, Grandpa, and then tell me about it.

Would you?

Pioneering...

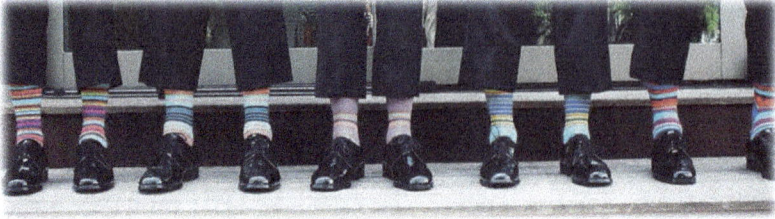

October 18

Guess what, God!

(Giggle, giggle, giggle.)

Grandpa has one blue sock and one black sock on.

Did he notice?
Did he mean to do that?

Has he ever gone a whole day with
two different colored socks on?

Well, okay.

I don't really know if he's wearing two
different socks—I suspect, though, that
he's at least wearing two socks.

Bless Grandpa's socks and the toes within!

October 19

Hey God,

Can we talk about something a little unusual?
What was it like for Grandpa to fall in love with
Grandma? I'd love to hear that story! I'm married
now, and enjoy sharing life with my companion.

What was that like for Grandpa? I never really
thought about my grandparents as lovers, but
surely they are. Grandpa and Grandma surely must
experience profound depth in their sharing.

Wonderment...

October 20

Master Adventurer,

Grandpa taught me how to enjoy nature. We took walks
together when we were camping, or out on the farm. Now
that I'm older, I enjoy taking my own walks in the woods.
It's peace-full to be in the trees and hear the birds or feel the
breeze. It's a good time for my heart and soul to re-align.

What does Grandpa discover when he walks?
Does he learn while he walks?
Celebrating Grandpa's walking adventures.

Walking...

October 21

Holy God,

Life is life. Grandpa grew up in a different time
period than I did. It's amazing that we can share
so many common threads in our lives—even
given the differences in lifetimes.

I'm grateful that my heart is open to having
Grandpa in it. He has his own place there.
(When she looked in her heart,
there was a place just for Grandpa.)

Someday I will draw a picture of his place in
my heart. I have to invent colors required
to represent his spot.

Smashingly...

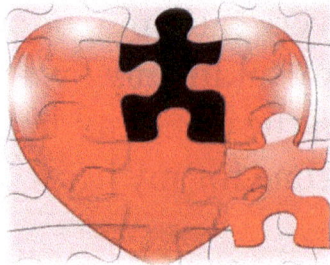

October 22

God of Man,

What is Grandpa's quest in life? When he was younger, I'm sure his quests were very different from what they are now.

As he seeks his own purpose in life, thank you for illuminating Grandpa's way to discovery.

Envisioning...

October 23

Radiant Father,

Your sunshine makes some interesting shadows and silhouettes. When I see my shadow, I pretend Grandpa's silhouette walks with me. We can walk together, even when we're apart.

Maybe Grandpa could dance with his shadow for a moment and pretend he's dancing with me. Or maybe his shadow could remind him you are walking with him.

Casting...

October 24

Splendid God,

Something amazing happens in autumn. The trees make beautiful colors when they are preparing to let go of their leaves. We can learn from the trees. When we let go of things we don't need anymore, we make ourselves beautiful, too.

Can you find an especially beautiful leaf for Grandpa to pick up today? He can bring it into his home and remember to let go of something he no longer needs.

Letting go...

October 25

Watchful Father,

When we moved Grandpa to an apartment, I kept one of his clocks. When I hear his clock announce the passing hours, I think about Grandpa. It's a pleasant reminder about all the times we have shared—I'm aware of his presence in my life.

Let Grandpa know that he's being thought about today.

Attentively...

October 26

Knock, knock, God.

It's me, again. How does Grandpa like to relax? Does he set aside a specific block of time—just to relax? When I pause to relax, I like to imagine a beautiful butterfly gently flying around me. It flutters around me from head to toe, leaving special relaxation dust.

I'd like to share my butterfly with Grandpa, if he'd invite him to come by for a spell.

Beautifully...

October 27

Well God,

I looked up an address to send a letter and realized all these names and addresses represent my friends and family. Grandpa probably has a long list of friends, too.

As I think about Grandpa's friends, I'm sending gratitude to them. I want to thank them for being Grandpa's friend.

As Grandpa thinks about his friends today, please remind him to be thankful. Bless Grandpa's friends.

Relationships...

October 28

Oh my, Lord.

I can't believe I ate the whole thing! I'm stuffed!

Does Grandpa ever eat too much?
Does he get that 'stuffed' feeling after an
enormous meal? I bet he is grate-full for
the opportunity to be well-fed.

I hope he remembers to be thankful when
his heart is full and well-fed, too.

Rejoicing...

October 29

Renewing Father,

I saw a lizard shedding his skin this morning.

It's a good reminder that when we grow and
change, we shed what is no longer useful for us.

There is always new skin for us to live
in when we shed the old one.

I hope Grandpa is comfortable in his skin.
If he isn't, could you please help him shed
what is no longer useful for him?

Grace-fully...

October 30

Extraordinary Lord,

Does Grandpa ever get the blahs?
What are blah days far? What are
you trying to tell us? If Grandpa has
a blah day, enlighten his path so he
can be peaceful with his blahs.

Ho, humming...

October 31

Trick or treat, Jesus!

Did Grandpa ever take his kids trick or
treating? I wonder how Grandpa dressed
up when he went door to door as a kid.

I'm stuffing Grandpa's bag full
of loving treats today.

Boo!

November 1

Hey you, God Being,

Does Grandpa ever buy flowers for himself? I do that sometimes, so I can remember how beautiful your world is.

There is so much beauty all around us. Not just flowers, but beautiful people, too.

Would it be okay for Grandpa to buy himself some flowers to enjoy? Then he can remember how beautiful he is to me.

Pondering...

November 2

God,

I'm having a bad hair day. Not only is my hair uncooperative, but it seems like nothing is going the way it's supposed to today.

I suspect Grandpa has a bad hair day now and then. When he's having one of those days, could you share some of that patience you shared with me?

Relentlessly...

November 3

Dear Father,

Thank you for medicine. Grandpa
takes medicine to keep things in
working order, now that he's older.

I'm grateful he's able to get what he
needs, and that we have medicine
to help us out as required.

Constantly...

November 4

What if, God?

Suppose Grandpa drank his soup out of the bowl, without
using a spoon. Perhaps he could pour his coffee in a bowl
instead of a cup. Let's do something unordinary today.

I'm going to eat my salad with my fingers today.

What if Grandpa did something wild and outrageous
today. Then, we can share our outrageous
adventures with each other.

Adventuring...

November 5

Blessed Father,

Rainy days make for good nap days. Does Grandpa ever take unscheduled naps on rainy days? Sometimes, I like to step out in the rain without an umbrella, just to feel the rain.

What sort of things does Grandpa do on rainy days?

Here's a towel...

November 6

Is Grandpa okay, God?

November 7

Holy Father,

Grandpa gets a little cough now and then, especially during the cold months.

I know he keeps candy corn around the house, because I always snitch a piece when I go visit him.

Grandpa always said that candy corn cured his cough.

Nurturing...

November 8

God,

Thanks for the reminder. I wonder what the reminder gift is all about. Reminders help us remember something.

What would we do if we didn't have reminders? Maybe we'd forget something that doesn't need to be remembered. That's a gracious gift, too.

Did Grandpa remember what you reminded him about today? Reminders are invitations. Thank you for reminder blessings.

Recalling...

November 9

Hey God,

Let's talk about the joy that comes from unexpected surprises. Sure. Sometimes surprises are less joyful than others. How do we find joy in what seems to be joyless?

I guess that's where the gift of choice comes in. May Grandpa's surprises be joy-full.

Surprise!

November 10

Now and then, God,

We can gather a slew of stuff over the course of a lifetime. Sometimes that stuff helps us remember things. Then, there's the stuff that fills up spaces. I know Grandpa has lots of stuff.

I wonder if you would point out a special something that would be a blessing for him today.

Lurking wonders...

November 11

Loving Father,

I want to wake something up in Grandpa's awareness. When he thinks about people, he does so unselfishly.

He gives his love for others so freely. Would you help him realize how amazingly unselfish he is?

Graciously...

November 12

Discovering One,

I was going through some of my family treasures and found something Grandpa gave me. I held it in my hand and close to my heart.

His heart feels close to mine as I remember the experiences associated with this treasure.

What treasure will Grandpa uncover today?

Cherishing...

November 13

Fostering Father,

I know that Grandpa's Dad has been in your care for many years. Does Grandpa ever miss talking with his father?

Would it be okay for him to write a letter to his father and put it in a special place so he can find it on another day?

Will Grandpa's Father hear his thoughts and prayers?

Connecting...

November 14

Everlasting Father,

You've given us senses—our eyes, ears, touch, taste and smell. Another of your awesome senses is the senses that come with the heart—joy, sadness, anger, health, excitement, love.

These senses are all blessings you've given us so that our life is rich and real somehow.

What is Grandpa sensing?

Is there something he sees, smells, tastes, or feels?

Thank you for giving him senses.

Mindfully...

November 15

Amazing Father,

Grandpas are miraculous. They are different than dads and they are different than siblings. Grandpas are important.

There are things only a Grandpa can do and things only a Grandpa can say. Grandpas are irreplaceable yet required.

Grandpas are truly miraculous.

Astounded...

November 16

Dear God,

New day. New gift. Days are amazing, unwrapped presents. You give them to us every single day! Unwrapped presents are so very special.

I hope Grandpa experiences today as a gift. When he gets out of bed, it's like stepping into a brand-new gift.

I hope he makes the most of it.

Choosing...

November 17

Vast and Powerful God,

Grandpa accomplished something awesome. He made a child that became my parent. When that happened, he turned into a Grandpa.

Isn't that an amazing accomplishment? Today, I'm celebrating Grandpa's awesome accomplishment.

Celebrating...

November 18

Delightful Spirit,

Does Grandpa's feet ever get a tickle? I remember sitting on Grandpa's lap, and he tickled my belly.

Sometimes you give us private tickles—just between me and thee. I hope the private tickle you give Grandpa today will make him giggle.

Cheerfully...

November 19

Guardian Lord,

Does Grandpa ever feel lost? I went on a hike and got lost once. I walked and walked and eventually found my way into familiar territory. It feels scary to be lost, especially if you're alone.

If Grandpa feels lost, perhaps you could help him find his way. You must always be with him because he always seems to find his way.

No, it might not be the way he thought he would go, but you always get him back on track.

Thank you for helping Grandpa to find his way.

Roving...

November 20

Beauteous One,

You know how much Grandpa loves
the moon. If there is a moon for him
to see this day or night, make it
especially glorious for him. Grandpa
tells me that God is in the moon.
You must be there to light our way
in our darkest hours.

Illuminating...

November 21

Revealing Savior,

I want to wake up Grandpa's tastebuds. I know.
It's an odd request. When Grandpa eats today,
maybe he could put on a blindfold or turn
all the lights off so it's dark.

Then he can feel around for his food. But, when
he eats, I bet his tastebuds wake up, and he
gets to experience something new.

Attentively...

November 22

Knowledgeable Father,

Sometimes saying goodbye feels sad.
I said goodbye to one of my violins today.
I'm sad.

That instrument and I shared many
moments in this life.

If Grandpa is saying goodbye to someone or
something, please walk with him.

Let him know it's okay to feel sad, and help
him see the magic in setting things free.

Splendor...

November 23

Wonderful Christ,

It feels good to experience kindness: from you, from other people, from our furry friends.

Does Grandpa still experience kindness?

I pray today that Grandpa finds unexpected kindnesses. Kind acts from different people, kind blessings from you—like the sun, or any gentle kindness that helps Grandpa's day to be full of blessings.

Gently...

November 24

Reverent Father,

Are you with Grandpa when he feels unmotivated? I bet if he stepped in a puddle (shoes on or off), his motivation would shift.

When Grandpa's unmotivated, please light a fire in his spirit so when the un-motivation is over, then he's ready to hit the ground running.

Shaking things up...

November 25

Gracious Savior,

I saw another lizard this morning. He was all perched up on a rock, looking for something. His patience is inspiring. You are one of the most patient beings! You watch over us as we navigate our lives. Sometimes, we learn quickly, with clarity. Other times we're not so speedy to catch the gist of the lesson.

If Grandpa is looking for something, could you give him patience? I'm sure he will find what he seeks. Sometimes patience is required to be rewarded.

Patiently...

November 26

Bountiful God,

This is a day we give thanks for
life, for love for food and home, for
safety and grace. I'm thankful for
my Grandpa—who he is, what he
is, and what that means to me.

Joyously...

November 27

Heavenly Father,

Let's talk about dew. In the early mornings, sometimes the earth has a blanket of sparkles as the sun glazes the grass. Maybe that's the earth's way of preparing for something miraculous.

Grandpa is like dew. When your sun falls upon him, he sparkles. Thank you for preparing miracles for us.

Preparing...

November 28

I'm curious, God,

What does Grandpa see when he looks in the mirror? Does he love what he sees? I hope so! What do other people see when they see Grandpa? I see wisdom, love, and loyalty when I see Grandpa.

When Grandpa sees himself in the mirror, help him see what I see, or what you see.

Reflections...

November 29

Tender Christ,

I remember a time when Grandpa
took my hand and guided me. His
hand felt safe and watchful.
He has amazing hands.

Do you ever hold Grandpa's hand
when he wants guidance? Can he
feel your amazing hand?

Sighing...

November 30

Oh, Holy Spirit,

I wonder what Grandpa feels when your wind
feels cold. I want to shelter myself from feeling
cold. Does Grandpa ever seek shelter from
something? If he does, would you help him?

If he is cold, let him know warmth and protection.
When he seeks shelter, help him feel secure.

Warm thoughts...

December 1

Hey Holy One,

I lit a candle today. The light from the flame feels warm.

Today I sensed that something new is on the horizon.
What advent is stirring today?
Open Grandpa's heart to your flame.

Bless him as he experiences something wondrous today.

Anticipating...

December 2

Enriching Lord,

What's Grandpa doing today? Are you with him?
Is Grandpa completing something today?

Maybe he's doing nothing. Perhaps he's thinking.

Did you give him some praise today?

Companions...

December 3

Subtle Spirit,

I'm fascinated by the colors produced by prisms. Did you make those so we can see all the lustrous colors that make up our lives? Grandpa is like a prism! When your light shines through him, a myriad of colors blast through.

Iridescence...

December 4

Glorious Lord,

It's interesting how we only have one March, one summer, and one December in a year. I hope Grandpa's December is full of your loving guidance.

Some things will seem the same to him—like other Decembers he's lived.

I hope there are new things for him in store for this December—unlike any other he's had before.

Inspirationally...

December 5

Durable God,

Before we had traffic signs, how did people know which way to go to get places? Did they just use what's in their hearts to find their way? I think they experimented and learned when to stop, when to go, and when to be cautious.

Did you help them? I hope you're still helping Grandpa follow the right signs.

What will his direction be?

Fervently...

December 6

Dear God,

Sometimes we think everyone has to be the same. That causes some interesting conflicts. I'm glad we're all unique. Grandpa wouldn't be who he is if his experiences were exactly the same as mine. I'm glad we're different, and I love him just the way he is.

He's the only Grandpa I have that is made just like he is. Thank you for making this marvelous gift— Grandpa. You've done a good job watching over him. Thank you for letting me be who I am with him.

Graciously...

December 7

Thank you, Father,

Thank you for happy food. What sort of food is happy for Grandpa? Cranberry bread is a happy food for me. It has a subtle sweetness and a refreshing zing all at the same time.

Would it be okay for Grandpa to have some happy food? I want to see his face soften when he bites into what makes him happy. Happy food not only tastes good, but it nourishes the soul.

Scrumptiously...

December 8

Spirit of Joy,

This year is just about out of days! Would it be okay to do something fun with Grandpa? I'll do this with him.

Put your right hand on your left shoulder. Hold it here, put your left hand on your right shoulder. Now squeeze.

We just gave each other a nice big hug. I'm pretending I'm hugging Grandpa. Who is Grandpa hugging?

Thank you for helping us learn about hugs. They feel good, even when I hug myself.

Lots of hugs...

December 9

Dong, dong, dong, God.

That's Grandpa's clock singing. Can you hear it? What time is it? Is it time for a breath of fresh air? Maybe it's time to do some reading.

Perhaps it's time to stop and remember how important Grandpa is to me.

Thank you for these clocks that sing. When I hear Grandpa's clock chime, I think about him. Bless Grandpa's memories when he hears that sound. Help him remember how important he is to me.

Exuberantly...

December 10

Caring Father,

How can I help Grandpa today? What am I going to do? Because he's there and I'm here, I'm going to send some thoughts his way. Let him know that I'm here for him.

I'm sprinkling magical stardust and sending it his way. Let the dust fall where it needs to so that it's just right for Grandpa.

Pitter, pat, pitter, pat...

December 11

Healing Father,

I'm not feeling too good today. I think some extra rest is in order. What does Grandpa do when he doesn't feel good? I hope you're there to let him know it won't last forever.

Maybe he's needing some extra tender loving care today. Whatever he needs, please let him receive what he's needing.

Mending...

December 12

Colorful Savior,

Sitting in front of a fireplace creates warmth, not only for my body but also in my heart. There are magical lessons in the firepit. The coals that fuel the fire.

The oxygen that feeds the fire. There are people in my life that help keep the fire burning in my heart.

Thank you for controlled fires to enjoy. They help me remember what makes my heart blaze brightly. What does Grandpa see in the fire?

Experimenting...

December 13

God,

I did some Christmas shopping today. I saw people scurrying around to get just the right gift for their loved ones.

Then I saw people helping others. This chaos is interesting to observe from different perspectives.

Are there some new perspectives Grandpa can have about this chaos? Maybe he needs a new perspective about something other than shopping.

Can you help him with that?
Open his mind to think about something in a new way.

Observing...

December 14

Shhhh.

You hear that? Hear that nothing sound?

Can you hear that there is quiet?

What peace will be Grandpa's, dear God?

What quiet will befall him?

Silently...

December 15

Dear God,

You must have an amazing Christmas tree. I imagine that each of your creations is a unique ornament, and all those unique ornaments light up your Christmas tree.

Oh! I think I spotted that Grandpa ornament over there—it looks just like my Grandpa.

I'm glad he has a place on your tree.

Decoratively...

December 16

Buoyant God,

Some people only find you in church, or in prayer. We think that's your place. I think you're always with us; whether we're sitting in our favorite chair, repairing a shingle, or even when we are enjoying fellowship with others.

What's Grandpa doing right now? Are you there with him?

Trajectories...

December 17

Watchful One,

What makes Grandpa feel safe? Are there special things he does to feel safe?

Sometimes (okay, usually) I sleep with lots of pillows to feel safe. Sometimes I hug a teddy bear to feel safe.

I know you are there to help him feel safe. Bless Grandpa's life so he feels safe.

Security...

December 18

Calling on God! Calling on God!

I did something fun today. I found
some Play-dough and made a face
that looks like Grandpa's face.
(Well, as best I could anyway.)

I'm putting his face right here on the
table, so I can see him any time I
want to. That way we can
talk every day, too.

Playfully...

December 19

Father,

We created this glue stuff. We use it to hold
things together. I think you have a special
glue that helps families stay together.

You know, Grandpa and I are different, but you
somehow keep us together with your special glue.

Bonding...

December 20

Hello God?

Does Grandpa ever hold his own hand?
When he holds his hands together today,
maybe he'll pretend I'm there with him to
hold his hand. Hands are good for holding.

I'm astonished at all the hands
his hands have touched.

Touching...

December 21

Faithful Father,

I have an idea. I'm making a list of all
the riches I have that don't cost
money. Look at all this wealth!

I bet if Grandpa made a list like this,
he'd be wonderfully surprised to
find out how wealthy he is.

Awareness...

December 22

Magnificent Christ,

Magnifying glasses are interesting. They help us see things. What would happen if Grandpa held a magnifying glass up to his face to see what's there. Would he see something he hasn't discovered before?

Oh, look at that. There's a wrinkle near his eye that happened because he smiled. What does Grandpa see in his face?

Uncanny...

December 23

Delightful Spirit...

I'm wondering about something. If the little boy that turned into my Grandpa had something he wanted to share with the man that is now my Grandpa, what would he want to share?

Can you help Grandpa hear the little boy inside of him?

Introspectively...

December 24

Wow God!

It's Christmas Eve. There's excitement in the air! Does Grandpa still feel like an excited child right before Christmas? Does he sense the anticipation of the birth of your son?

What does Grandpa anticipate during this special time? Maybe he'll put out some milk and cookies so he can feel like a kid again.

Eagerly...

December 25

Heavenly Father,

There is special wonderment about today. It feels different than other days.

This day brings a focus we don't have on other days of the year. It makes the world feel good.

Merry Christmas.

December 26

...Thank you.

December 27

Gracious God,

What inspires Grandpa? When I see children play, I feel inspired. Sometimes reading the words people have carefully put together to make a storybook inspires me.

I find inspiration when I listen to others.

Can you enlighten something inspiring for Grandpa today?

Igniting...

December 28

Great Father

Does Grandpa ever do anything or give something to someone for no reason? I know he does. He shares his love with me every day.

What a special gift to have Grandpa in my life.

Today I'm sharing a story about Grandpa with a friend. What is Grandpa giving or sharing today?

As always...

December 29

God,

Does Grandpa ever take a day off?
What does a chill-out day look
like for Grandpa? Does he wear
his pajamas all day long?
Maybe he takes naps all day.

Maybe he watches football or just
spends the whole day reading.
Is there a day when he can be a
couch potato if he wants to be?

Bursting...

December 30

Almighty God,

Sometimes my mind is buzzing around so ferociously that sleep is a challenge to acquire. Do you suppose Grandpa ever has a hard time falling asleep at night?

When Grandpa has a rest-less night, bring him solace so that rest-full sleep finds him.

Patiently...

December 31

Holy Father,

WOW! It's the last day of this year. Tomorrow will be the start of a brand new year.

Thank you for all the unique gifts we've had in every single day this year. I hope Grandpa has enjoyed sharing these prayers with me every day.

Thank you for hearing our prayers and for always being there to receive them and act on them.

In awe of your greatness...

Alexis Faere
Life Writes

AlexisFaere.com

Author, Blogger, Speaker, and Emotions Champion

Alexis Faere is an enchanting storyteller, writer, and whimsical spirit who weaves tales of magic and wonder. Her spiritual journey is shaped by her upbringing as a preacher's kid, where she quietly absorbed the profound truths and spiritual practices surrounding her daily life.

Today she shares her reflections and insights, offering these loving expressions to others, to deepen and strengthen a grandchild's connection with a grandparent. In addition to *Graceful Whispers*, be sure to see the companion book of prayers for Grandma, *Whispers of Love*. Alexis is also the author of an insight-packed series of emotional journal workbooks, a blog (AlexisFaere.com), and soon-to-be-released memoir.

Whether she is penning a prayer or stories, Alexis' words carry a timeless quality, resonating with readers of all ages. She invites readers on a transformative journey, drawing from her deep-rooted spirituality, personal reflections, and her passion to encourage emotional maturity and rich connections with people.

A Review Please

As an author, I know how important reviews are for getting the word out about my books. When readers leave a review on Amazon or any other bookstores, it helps others discover my book and decide whether it's right for them.

Plus, it gives me feedback on what readers enjoyed and what they didn't.

So, if you've read my book and enjoyed it (or even if you didn't!), I would really appreciate it if you would take a moment to leave a review on Amazon.

It doesn't have to be long or complicated. Just leave a few words about what you thought of my book would be incredibly helpful.

Thank you so much!

www.ingramcontent.com/pod-product-compliance
Lightning Source LLC
Chambersburg PA
CBHW080417030426
42335CB00020B/2488